CONTENTS

Introduction   4

Dinner Party Solutions   8

Classics with a Twist   32

No Time to Cook   56

Slim for Life   82

World Food   106

Al Fresco   138

Celebrations   168

Notes on Ingredients   188

Index   190

Acknowledgements   192

INTRODUCTION

Vegetarian Supercook is about real food for real people. When planning the book, I, and all the team involved, wanted it to be different from other vegetarian cookery books. So we conducted our own 'straw poll' and asked all the vegetarians we could find what they wanted in a vegetarian cookery book – they told us, and this book is the result.

Help with 'dinner parties' – entertaining friends – came top of the list, so the book opens with Dinner Party Solutions, containing easy yet impressive recipes that are popular with vegetarians and meat-eaters alike – carnivores will not miss their meat when you offer them these. I've expanded further on the theme of entertaining, this time in a more seasonal way, with the chapter entitled Celebrations, because ideas for Christmas and Thanksgiving, for spring, summer and autumn feasts also came high on the wish list. And talking of summer, the perennial question of what to cook at vegetarian barbecues was asked. So this is included in the Al Fresco section, along with recipes for brunches and informal parties – in the sunshine, let's hope.

One of the reasons I love doing book-signings and cookery demonstrations is the opportunity to talk to people. What they've told me makes me realize that just about everyone also wants recipes for weekday suppers when they're too tired and pressed for time to cook; they also need recipes for losing weight and keeping slim – me included! So these chapters were added to the list – and I hope they'll help.

Then, because many of our most delectable vegetarian dishes have their roots in other cuisines – those of India, Thailand and the Middle East, for instance, where meat-free cookery has been practised for centuries and is, in some places, the normal way of eating – I wanted to include some of these delicious dishes, so the chapter World Food went in.

Finally, having been living, eating and breathing the world of vegetarian cookery all my life, I decided to have some fun. No, I couldn't face the thought of hummus, chilli, ratatouille or lasagne again, either, but recognized that they definitely have something going for them, or they wouldn't still be around. So I've devised new ways with them – and we have the Classics with a Twist chapter.

If I have one wish for this book, it's that it will encourage more people to have a go at cooking. It's easy and it's fun. I had no inhibitions when I first started playing around in my parents' kitchen when I was about

Rose Elliot
Vegetarian Supercook

First published in Great Britain in 2004 by Hamlyn, a division
of Octopus Publishing Group Ltd
2–4 Heron Quays, London E14 4JP

First published in paperback in 2006

Distributed in the United States and Canada by
Sterling Publishing Co., Inc.
387 Park Avenue South, New York, NY 10016-8810

ISBN-13: 978-0-600-61421-0
ISBN-10: 0-600-61421-2

A CIP catalogue record for this book
is available from the British Library

Printed and bound in China

10 9 8 7 6 5 4 3 2

Notes

Both metric and imperial measurements are given for the
recipes. Use one set of measures only, not a mixture of both.

Ovens should be preheated to the specified temperature.
If using a fan-assisted oven, follow the manufacturer's
instructions for adjusting the temperature. This usually
means reducing the temperature by 20°C (65°F).
Grills should also be preheated.

Free-range medium eggs should be used unless otherwise
specified. The Department of Health advises that eggs should
not be consumed raw. This book contains some dishes made
with raw or lightly cooked eggs. It is prudent for more
vulnerable people, such as pregnant and nursing mothers,
invalids, the elderly, babies and young children, to avoid
uncooked or lightly cooked dishes made with eggs.

Buy cheese with the vegetarian symbol to ensure it is made
with vegetarian rennet and buy vegetarian parmesan-style
cheese instead of traditional Parmesan which is not
vegetarian. Always check the labels of preprepared
ingredients to make sure they do not contain
non-vegetarian ingredients such as gelatine.

www.vegsoc.org

Vegan recipes are labelled Ⓥ

This book includes dishes made with nuts and nut
derivatives. It is advisable for those with known allergic
reactions to nuts and nut derivatives and those who may
be potentially vulnerable to these allergies, such as pregnant
and nursing mothers, invalids, the elderly, babies and children,
to avoid dishes made with nuts and nut oils. It is also prudent
to check the labels of preprepared ingredients for the
possible inclusion of nut derivatives.

Fresh herbs should be used unless otherwise stated.
If unavailable use dried herbs as an alternative but halve
the quantities stated.

nine, trying to follow a recipe. I thought that the big numbers on the scale were ounces, not pounds, so the sponge cake I was trying to make, requiring four ounces of flour (thank goodness it was just four!) needed the largest mixing bowl in the cupboard and all the flour in the house. It was just as well my mother came into the kitchen before I got too far. She put me right – and I can remember feeling embarrassed – but she didn't discourage me or make me feel stupid, and I think my joy of cooking grew from that moment.

I was making meals by the time I was 12, and then cooking for about 30 people – visitors to the retreat centre run by my family – on a daily basis by the time I was 16. I feel so thankful that I had the chance to experiment in the kitchen when I was young enough not to worry about making mistakes. It felt like playing and it still does today, when I'm working on a book – creating and testing recipes, mixing colours, flavours and textures in my kitchen, with the door closed. I like to be completely on my own, a cafetière of coffee on the table, the air warm and fragrant with onions, garlic and spices. It seems to me that this sense of fun and passion is one of the secrets of cooking – that and a natural love of food. I always think that American columnist Harriet Van Horne expressed it perfectly when she said: 'Cooking is like love – it should be entered into with abandon, or not at all.'

Anyone can learn to cook, and at least you can eat your 'mistakes', so you don't waste much! Speed and confidence come with practice and they're worth acquiring because, like anything else, the better you get, the more enjoyable it becomes. As for judging flavourings, and the 'doneness' of food such as pasta, rice and vegetables – things that I know bother people, I say cook to please yourself, not some critical member of the 'food police' sitting on your shoulder. Try things this way, try them that way; find out what works for you and what doesn't; discover what you like best. Taste a dish as you go along and feel free to make it taste right for you. After all, you're the one who's going to eat it, not the writer of the recipe. As far as this writer is concerned, I just want you to have fun making the food and enjoy eating it. If you want to change a recipe to suit the particular ingredients available or your own taste preferences, that's absolutely fine. Be your own Supercook.

If you're a parent, do encourage your kids to cook with you – it's such a valuable life skill. One of my daughters recently told me about a colleague who was finding it difficult to follow a vegetarian diet. 'She doesn't know how to cook so she can't just rustle something up in the kitchen. If she can't find what she's looking for in the "ready meals" section, she's stuck.' This was said without criticism, as though it was quite an unremarkable situation. Well, I find it sad when I think of the amount of pleasure, nutrition, creativity and money that are lost as a result of not being able to cook. The recipes in this book offer a solution to anyone who thinks they can't cook. They are easily put together, made with readily available ingredients and I hope they'll inspire anyone to create home-cooked food.

I like to use organic produce wherever I can because I believe food is better for you when it's grown as naturally as possible, without artificial fertilizers and chemical sprays. I think it tastes better, but most of all, and I hope you won't think I'm daft saying this, I find it 'feels' more full of life and energy when you prepare and eat it, and it is also undoubtedly better for the ecology of our planet. If you haven't tried organic produce already, a good way to start is to make a habit of buying something organic every time you shop. I truly believe that home cooking, based on good, healthy ingredients really does contribute to our health, both physical and emotional. A meal created with love, eaten by everyone together, relaxing around the table, chatting, laughing, sharing: how truly nurturing that is.

My kitchen is on the small side and I'm a little untidy so, for me, some sense of organization is essential. I find it helps to have the equipment I use all the time out on my work surface, ready for immediate action, rather than in a cupboard waiting to be taken out and assembled. I have three absolute favourites: a very heavy, generously sized wooden chopping board, a sharp steel knife I've had for years and a large food processor. I think it's worth spending money on all these things, but particularly on a good knife, because it saves so much time and effort. My advice is to go to a good kitchen shop, ask for guidance and try a few in your hand to see whether you like the feel. Then there are my electric citrus squeezer, electric whisk and olive-stoner, and I've just discovered the usefulness of a fine microplane grater for things like garlic and ginger.

So, these are the things that help me, but everyone has to find their own way of working, one that feels harmonious and right for them and makes food preparation a pleasure. Once you're organized, vegetarian cooking is particularly rewarding because the raw ingredients are so beautiful to look at, to touch and to taste, just brimming with life force, especially if they are organic.

I do hope that you'll feel this joy as you read and use this book and that you will find the recipes fun, inspiring and wonderful to eat.

Rose Elliot

DINNER PARTY SOLUTIONS

By 'dinner party' I mean those times when you want to cook something extra special for family or friends, and to share warmth, conviviality and laughter. My favourite place for entertaining is in my kitchen, with the lights dimmed and the candles lit.

These recipes may take a little longer and cost a little more to make, but they're not difficult. Make life easy for yourself by having a simple first course – something cold, or a soup – and a pudding that can be prepared in advance, then all you need to think about is the main course – and enjoying yourself!

Iced beetroot soup

PREPARATION 25 MINUTES COOKING 30–40 MINUTES SERVES 6

I TABLESPOON OLIVE OIL • I LARGE ONION, CHOPPED • I LARGE POTATO, PEELED AND CUT INTO SMALL CUBES • 750g (1½lb) COOKED BEETROOT (NOT IN VINEGAR), ROUGHLY DICED • PARED RIND OF ½ LEMON • 1.5 litres (2½ pints) WATER OR LIGHT VEGETABLE STOCK • 2 TABLESPOONS LEMON JUICE • SALT AND PEPPER • SOURED CREAM, COARSELY GROUND BLACK PEPPER AND CHOPPED CHIVES, DILL OR MINT, TO SERVE

1 Heat the olive oil in a large saucepan, add the onion and fry for 10 minutes, until soft but not brown, then add the potato, cover the pan and cook gently for a further 5 minutes.

2 Add the beetroot, lemon rind and the water or vegetable stock. Bring to the boil, then cover and simmer for 15–20 minutes, or until the potato is soft.

3 Purée the mixture in a food processor or blender until perfectly smooth. If you prefer an even smoother texture, pass the mixture through a sieve into a large bowl.

4 Add the lemon juice and season with salt and pepper to taste. Chill until required, then taste and adjust the seasoning if necessary.

5 To serve, ladle the soup into chilled bowls and top with a spoonful of soured cream, some coarsely ground black pepper and chopped herbs of your choice.

This soup, which you can also serve hot if you prefer, brought me a marriage proposal. It's particularly effective served in bowls sitting in outer bowls of crushed ice.

Puffy aubergine pancakes with red pepper purée

PREPARATION 40 MINUTES COOKING I HOUR SERVES 6

I LARGE AUBERGINE • I LARGE RED PEPPER • 2 TABLESPOONS OLIVE OIL • I LARGE ONION, FINELY CHOPPED • 4 LARGE GARLIC CLOVES, FINELY CHOPPED • I EGG • 2 TABLESPOONS FINE WHOLEMEAL FLOUR • 2 TEASPOONS CHOPPED OREGANO • OLIVE OIL FOR SHALLOW-FRYING • SALT AND PEPPER • OREGANO LEAVES OR SMALL SPRIGS AND COARSELY GROUND BLACK PEPPER, TO GARNISH

1 Remove the stem from the aubergine. Put the aubergine and pepper on a baking sheet and roast in a preheated oven, 200°C (400°F), Gas Mark 6, for about 30 minutes, or until both are very tender when pierced with a sharp knife. Allow to cool. This can be done in advance when the oven is on for something else if convenient. You won't need the oven any more unless you want to make the pancakes straightaway and keep them warm for a short time before serving.

2 Meanwhile, heat the olive oil in a saucepan, add the onion, cover and cook gently for 10 minutes, or until the onion is tender. Add the garlic, cook for 1–2 minutes longer, then remove from the heat.

3 Make the red pepper purée. Pull the papery outer skin from the cooled pepper, scoop out the seeds and core from the inside and discard the stem if still attached. Put the pepper into a food processor or blender with half the onion and garlic mixture and whiz to a thick purée. Season with salt and pepper and put to one side.

4 Rinse out the food processor and put in the roasted aubergine, the remaining onion and garlic mixture, the egg, flour, oregano and some salt and pepper to taste. Whiz to a thick batter.

5 Just before you want to serve the pancakes, heat 2.5mm (⅛ inch) depth of olive oil in a frying pan. When it's hot enough for a tiny speck of the batter to sizzle as soon as it hits the oil, put in heaped teaspoons of the batter mixture. Fry on one side for about 2 minutes, then flip them over and fry the other side. Take them out and put on to a plate lined with kitchen paper. Repeat until you have 18 little pancakes and all the mixture has been used up.

6 Just before serving, gently reheat the red pepper purée. Put three pancakes on each serving plate and top each pancake with a spoonful of the red pepper purée. Garnish with oregano leaves or a sprig and some coarsely ground black pepper. Serve at once.

Twice-baked cheese soufflés on mushroom steaks

PREPARATION 40 MINUTES COOKING 20 MINUTES SERVES 6

BUTTER FOR GREASING • 250g (8oz) LOW-FAT SOFT CREAM CHEESE • 4 EGG YOLKS • I50g (5oz) STRONG
CHEDDAR CHEESE, GRATED • 5 EGG WHITES • 150ml (¼ pint) DOUBLE CREAM • 50g (2oz) FRESHLY GRATED
PARMESAN CHEESE • SALT AND PEPPER
MUSHROOM STEAKS I TABLESPOON OLIVE OIL • I5g (½oz) BUTTER • 6 FIELD OR PORTOBELLO MUSHROOMS,
STEMS REMOVED

1 Grease 6 x 150ml (¼ pint) capacity ramekins, old cups or individual pudding moulds generously with butter.

2 Put the cream cheese into a bowl with the egg yolks and beat until smooth, then add the Cheddar and season generously with salt and pepper. Whisk the egg whites with a clean, grease-free whisk until they are standing in stiff peaks. Stir a heaped tablespoon into the egg yolk mixture to loosen it, then gently fold in the remaining whisked egg whites. Spoon the mixture into the greased ramekins, cups or moulds: it can come level with the top, but don't pile it any higher.

3 Stand the ramekins in a roasting tin and pour in boiling water to come halfway up the sides. Bake in a preheated oven, 180°C (350°F), Gas Mark 4, for 15 minutes, until the soufflés are risen and set. Remove from the oven and leave to get cold – they'll sink a bit.

4 Meanwhile, prepare the mushroom steaks. Heat the olive oil and butter in a frying pan, add the mushrooms and fry on both sides until tender – about 5 minutes in all. Place them, black side up, in a shallow casserole dish from which you can serve them at the table.

5 Loosen the edges of the soufflés and turn out on to your hand, then put one on top of each mushroom in the casserole dish. Spoon the cream over and around them and scatter the Parmesan on top. They can now wait until you are ready to bake them.

6 Bake the mushrooms and soufflés in a preheated oven, 220°C (425°F), Gas Mark 7, for 15–20 minutes, or until the soufflés are puffed up and golden and the Parmesan on top is crunchy.

Goats' cheese and cranberry parcels

PREPARATION 15 MINUTES COOKING 15–20 MINUTES SERVES 4

4 SHEETS FILO PASTRY, 40 X 23cm (16 X 9 inches) • 2 X 100g (3½oz) CYLINDRICAL GOATS' CHEESES

• 3–4 TABLESPOONS OLIVE OIL • 4 HEAPED TEASPOONS CRANBERRY SAUCE

1 Cut each piece of filo into 4 quarters. Cut the cheeses in half widthways.

2 To make a parcel, put one of the pieces of filo on a work surface and brush with olive oil. Put another piece over it at right angles to make a cross and brush with olive oil again. Lay a third piece diagonally, as if you were making a star shape, brush with oil, then top with the final piece, diagonally, to complete the 'star', and brush with oil.

3 Place one of the pieces of cheese, cut-side up, in the centre of the pastry and put a heaped teaspoon of cranberry sauce on top of it. Fold up the sides of the filo and scrunch them at the top so they hold together. Brush all over with olive oil. Make three more parcels in the same way.

4 Place all the parcels on a lightly oiled baking sheet and bake in a preheated oven, 200°C (400°F), Gas Mark 6, for 15–20 minutes, or until crisp and lightly browned. Serve at once with a leafy salad dressed with vinaigrette – I think a chicory and watercress salad goes well as the bitterness contrasts with the sweet cranberry sauce. Alternatively, if you have the time to prepare them, some creamy mashed potatoes and fine green beans go well with the parcels.

Sweet potato and wild rice patties with lime salsa

PREPARATION 30 MINUTES COOKING 1 HOUR SERVES 6

6 SWEET POTATOES, ABOUT 250g (8oz) EACH • 300g (10oz) MIXED BASMATI AND WILD RICE • 6–8 SPRING ONIONS, CHOPPED • 2 TABLESPOONS GRATED FRESH ROOT GINGER • 8 GARLIC CLOVES, CRUSHED • 175g (6oz) CASHEW NUTS, GRATED • DRY POLENTA FOR COATING • OLIVE OIL FOR SHALLOW-FRYING • SALT AND PEPPER • COOKED CAVALO NERO, KALE OR SPINACH, TO SERVE

SALSA PARED RIND AND CHOPPED FLESH OF 1 LIME • 4 TABLESPOONS CHOPPED CORIANDER LEAVES • 1 TABLESPOON DESICCATED COCONUT • 1 GREEN CHILLI, DESEEDED AND CHOPPED

1 Make a cut in the sweet potatoes, to let out the steam, place them on a baking sheet and bake in a preheated oven, 230°C (450°F), Gas Mark 8, for 50–60 minutes, or until they feel tender to the point of a knife. Remove from the oven and allow to cool a little. This can be done in advance if convenient.

2 Meanwhile, cook the rice. Bring a large pan of water to the boil, add the rice, bring back to the boil, then leave to simmer for 15–20 minutes, or until the rice is tender. It can be a little on the soft side for this recipe. Drain into a colander, rinse with cold water, drain again thoroughly and put into a bowl.

3 Scoop the sweet potato flesh out of the skins and add to the rice, along with the spring onions, ginger, garlic and cashews. Season with salt and pepper.

4 Form the mixture into 12 flat patties and coat with polenta, then set aside until required.

5 To make the salsa, simply mix all the ingredients together and set aside.

6 Just before you want to serve the meal, pour enough olive oil into a frying pan to coat the bottom very lightly. Heat until smoking, then add some of the patties. Fry until browned and crisp on one side, then turn them over and fry the second side, adding a little more olive oil as necessary. Lift them out carefully and put on to a baking sheet lined with kitchen paper. Keep them warm in the oven while you fry the rest.

7 Bring 2.5cm (1 inch) depth of water to the boil in a saucepan, add the cavalo nero, kale or spinach, cover and cook for 6–7 minutes, or until tender. Drain and season with salt and pepper.

8 Top each patty with a little of the salsa and serve with the greens – either all spread out on a large platter, the patties on top of the greens, or on individual plates.

I love the contrast between the bitter green leaves and the sweet patties – if you can't get cavalo nero, use kale or spinach instead.

Crunchy hazelnut croquettes with red onion marmalade

PREPARATION 30 MINUTES COOKING 1 HOUR SERVES 6

50g (2oz) BUTTER • 1 SMALL ONION, FINELY CHOPPED • 50g (2oz) FINE WHOLEMEAL FLOUR •
450ml (¾ pint) SOYA MILK • 1 TABLESPOON CHOPPED MIXED THYME AND OREGANO • 125g (4oz) HAZELNUTS,
FINELY GROUND • ½ TEASPOON YEAST EXTRACT • 250g (8oz) TALEGGIO CHEESE, RIND REMOVED • 1 EGG,
BEATEN • DRY POLENTA FOR COATING • OLIVE OIL FOR SHALLOW-FRYING • SALT AND PEPPER • OREGANO
OR THYME SPRIGS, TO GARNISH
RED ONION MARMALADE 1 TABLESPOON OLIVE OIL • 500g (1lb) RED ONIONS, THINLY SLICED • 1 TABLESPOON
SUGAR • 1½ TABLESPOONS SHERRY (ANY TYPE) OR RED WINE • 1 TABLESPOON RED WINE VINEGAR

1 To make the red onion marmalade, heat the olive oil in a large saucepan, add the onions, cover the pan and cook for about 15 minutes, stirring every 5 minutes, until very tender.

2 When the onions are very soft, add the sugar, sherry or wine and the vinegar and let the mixture simmer gently, uncovered, for about 30 minutes until it is thick and sticky with hardly any liquid left. Remove from the heat, season and cool if not using immediately.

3 Meanwhile, make the nut mixture, which needs to be done in advance and cooled before moulding the croquettes. Melt the butter in a large saucepan, add the onion, cover the pan and fry gently for about 7 minutes, until tender. Stir in the flour and cook for 2–3 minutes, but don't let it brown, then pour in the soya milk and stir over the heat until very thick. Remove from the heat, stir in the herbs, hazelnuts and yeast extract and add salt and pepper to taste. Spread out on a plate and leave to get completely cold.

4 When cold, divide the nut mixture into 6 and cut the cheese into 6 pieces. Take a piece of cheese and completely encase it in nut mixture, then dip it first into beaten egg and then into the polenta, to coat completely. Make 5 more croquettes in the same way.

5 Just before serving, reheat the onion marmalade if you've made it in advance. Fry the croquettes in a shallow depth of hot olive oil on both sides until crisp and golden brown, then drain on kitchen paper. Garnish with the herbs and serve with the red onion marmalade.

Chestnut-stuffed onions with porcini gravy

PREPARATION 30 MINUTES COOKING 40–50 MINUTES SERVES 6

6 LARGE ONIONS • I TABLESPOON OLIVE OIL, PLUS EXTRA FOR BRUSHING • I5g (½oz) BUTTER • I CELERY HEART, CHOPPED • 4–6 GARLIC CLOVES, FINELY CHOPPED • 3 X 275g (9oz) CANS VACUUM-PACKED WHOLE CHESTNUTS • I TABLESPOON CHOPPED THYME • 2 TABLESPOONS DRY POLENTA • SALT AND PEPPER • THYME SPRIGS, TO GARNISH

GRAVY I5g (½oz) DRIED PORCINI MUSHROOMS • 750ml (1¼ pints) VEGETABLE STOCK • I ONION, CHOPPED • 2 TABLESPOONS OLIVE OIL • 4 GARLIC CLOVES, FINELY CHOPPED • 2 TABLESPOONS FINE WHOLEMEAL FLOUR • 2 TABLESPOONS SOY SAUCE • 2 TABLESPOONS MADEIRA • SALT AND PEPPER

1 Cut the onions in half horizontally and trim them slightly if necessary to make them stand level. Using a sharp knife, cut out most of the centres, leaving about 3 good layers on the outside (as pictured). Brush these onion 'cups' all over with olive oil and place in a shallow casserole dish.

2 Chop the scooped-out onion. Heat the olive oil and butter in a large saucepan, add the chopped onion, celery and garlic, cover the pan and cook gently without browning for 10–15 minutes, or until tender. Remove from the heat.

3 Add the chestnuts to the onion mixture in the pan, mashing them a bit, then stir in the thyme and polenta and add salt and pepper to taste. Divide the mixture between the onion 'cups', heaping it up well, and bake in a preheated oven, 200°C (400°F), Gas Mark 6, for 30–35 minutes, until the onion 'cups' are tender – cover the casserole dish with foil if the stuffing seems to be drying out before this.

4 While the onions are cooking, make the gravy. Put the mushrooms into a saucepan with the vegetable stock. Bring to the boil, then cover and leave to soak for 15–20 minutes. Strain, reserving the liquid. Chop the mushrooms finely.

5 Fry the onion in the olive oil for 10 minutes, until tender and lightly browned. Add the chopped mushrooms and garlic, and fry for a further 1–2 minutes, then stir in the flour and cook to brown it a little. Pour in the reserved porcini liquid, the soy sauce and Madeira and stir over the heat until thickened.

6 For a really smooth sauce, you can now purée the whole lot in a food processor or blender (or strain it through a sieve) or, if you prefer some texture, leave it as it is.

7 Leave the gravy to simmer gently for 10 minutes, then add salt and pepper to taste. Serve the stuffed onions with the porcini gravy.

Using polenta here instead of traditional breadcrumbs keeps the stuffing moist while preventing it from getting soggy.

Croustade of asparagus hollandaise

PREPARATION 30 MINUTES COOKING 20–25 MINUTES SERVES 6

1kg (2lb) ASPARAGUS TIPS (THIN IF POSSIBLE), TRIMMED

CROUSTADE 150g (5oz) SOFT WHITE BREADCRUMBS • 150g (5oz) CASHEW NUTS, FINELY GROUND IN A COFFEE

GRINDER (OR USE GROUND ALMONDS) • 150g (5oz) BUTTER • 3 GARLIC CLOVES, FINELY CHOPPED •

75g (3oz) ONION, FINELY GRATED • 150g (5oz) PINE NUTS • 5 TEASPOONS WATER

HOLLANDAISE SAUCE 250g (8oz) BUTTER, CUT INTO CHUNKS • 4 EGG YOLKS • 2 TABLESPOONS LEMON JUICE •

SALT AND PEPPER

1 First make the croustade. Mix together the breadcrumbs, ground nuts, butter, garlic and onion, by hand or by whizzing in a food processor, then stir in the pine nuts and water and mix to make a dough.

2 Press the mixture down lightly into the base of a 30cm (12 inch) shallow oven-proof or pizza dish. Bake in a preheated oven, 200°C (400°F), Gas Mark 6, for 15–20 minutes, until crisp and golden brown. Set aside.

3 Cook the asparagus in a little boiling water for 3–4 minutes, or until tender, then drain.

4 Meanwhile, make the sauce. Melt the butter gently in a saucepan without browning it. Put the egg yolks, lemon juice and some seasoning into a food processor or blender and whiz for 1 minute until thick. With the motor running, pour in the melted butter in a thin, steady stream – the sauce will thicken. Let it stand for a minute or two.

5 Pile the asparagus on top of the croustade, pour the sauce over and serve at once.

To save yourself a last minute rush when you're expecting guests, you can make the base in advance and refrigerate or even freeze it, either before or after baking.

Tomato, pesto and mozzarella tart with walnut pastry

PREPARATION 30 MINUTES COOKING 1¾ HOURS SERVES 6

375g (12oz) FINE WHOLEMEAL FLOUR OR HALF WHOLEMEAL, HALF WHITE • 175g (6oz) BUTTER, CUT INTO ROUGH CHUNKS • ½ TEASPOON SALT • 50g (2oz) WALNUTS, FINELY CHOPPED • 3 TABLESPOONS COLD WATER • 2 TABLESPOONS OLIVE OIL

FILLING 1.1kg (2¼lb) BABY TOMATOES ON THE VINE • 1 TABLESPOON BALSAMIC VINEGAR • 1 RED ONION, SLICED • 1 TABLESPOON OLIVE OIL • 4 GARLIC CLOVES, SLICED • 4 TEASPOONS PESTO • 150g (5oz) MOZZARELLA CHEESE, DRAINED AND CUT INTO 1cm (½ inch) PIECES • 12 BLACK OLIVES, PREFERABLY KALAMATA • SALT AND PEPPER

1 Take the tomatoes off the vine and put them into a roasting tin. Pour the balsamic vinegar over them and bake in a preheated oven, 200°C (400°F), Gas Mark 6, for 45–50 minutes, or until they are bursting and blackened in places.

2 Meanwhile, make the pastry. Put the flour, butter and salt into a food processor and whiz until the mixture resembles coarse breadcrumbs. Alternatively, put the ingredients into a bowl and rub the butter into the flour with your fingertips. Add the walnuts and water and mix to a dough.

3 Turn the dough out on a lightly floured surface and knead briefly, then shape into a circle and roll out to fit a 28–30cm (11–12 inch) shallow round flan tin. Trim the edges, prick the base thoroughly all over, then chill for 30 minutes.

4 Continue with the filling: fry the onion in the olive oil for 10–15 minutes, until soft and sweet. Add the garlic and remove from the heat.

5 Bake the tart in the oven at the same temperature as for the tomatoes for 20 minutes, until the pastry is 'set' and lightly browned. A minute or two before you take it out of the oven, heat the remaining 2 tablespoons of olive oil in a small saucepan until smoking hot. As soon as the tart comes out of the oven, pour the hot olive oil all over the base – it will sizzle and almost 'fry'. This will 'waterproof' the base of the tart so that it will remain crisp.

6 Just before you want to serve the tart, put onion mixture and the roasted tomatoes in the tart case. Season with salt and pepper, remembering that both the pesto and the mozzarella are salty. Drizzle with pesto, then arrange the mozzarella and olives on top. Bake in a preheated oven, 180°C (350°F), Gas Mark 4, for 25 minutes, or until the mozzarella has melted and browned in places.

The reason for using tomatoes on the vine is for flavour rather than appearance, although they do look especially attractive in this tart.

Pea and mint timbales with baby vegetables and Parmesan crisps

PREPARATION 40 MINUTES COOKING 1¼ HOURS SERVES 6

15g (½oz) BUTTER, MELTED • 1–2 TABLESPOONS FINELY GRATED PARMESAN CHEESE • 500g (1lb) FROZEN PETITS POIS • 4 TABLESPOONS CHOPPED MINT • 150ml (¼ pint) DOUBLE CREAM • 200ml (7fl oz) SINGLE CREAM • 2 EGG YOLKS • 4 EGGS • GRATED NUTMEG • SALT AND PEPPER

PARMESAN CRISPS 3 TABLESPOONS FINELY GRATED PARMESAN CHEESE

BRAISED VEGETABLES 1 TABLESPOON OLIVE OIL • 25g (1oz) BUTTER • 500g (1lb) BABY CARROTS • 500g (1lb) TINY NEW POTATOES • 250g (8oz) PREPARED BABY FENNEL • 75ml (3fl oz) WATER • 125g (4oz) EACH ASPARAGUS TIPS, SUGAR-SNAP PEAS AND PODDED BROAD BEANS

1 Prepare 6 x 150ml (¼ pint) individual pudding bowls by brushing generously with melted butter, then dusting liberally with Parmesan.

2 To make the timbales, cook the peas and half the mint in boiling water for 2–3 minutes, or until tender. Drain then whiz to a purée in a food processor with the two lots of cream. Add the egg yolks and whole eggs and whiz again. Pour the mixture into a sieve set over a bowl and push through as much as you can – discard the residue. Season with nutmeg, salt and pepper, then pour into the prepared bowls.

3 Put the bowls in a deep roasting tin and pour in boiling water to come halfway up the sides. Bake in a preheated oven, 180°C (350°F), Gas Mark 4, for 40–45 minutes, or until a skewer inserted into the centre comes out clean. Remove and set aside.

4 To make the crisps, line a baking sheet with nonstick baking paper. Put ½ tablespoon of the Parmesan on the paper and spread it into a 7cm (3 inch) circle. Repeat to make 5 more circles of cheese. Increase the oven temperature to 200°C (400°F), Gas Mark 6, and bake for about 5 minutes, or until the Parmesan is golden brown and crisp. Leave to cool.

5 Next, cook the vegetables. Heat the olive oil and butter in a large saucepan and add the carrots, potatoes, fennel and water. Bring to the boil, cover and simmer for 15 minutes. Add the asparagus, sugar-snaps and broad beans, and simmer for a further 10 minutes, until all the vegetables are very tender. Season with salt and pepper.

6 Arrange the vegetables on warmed individual plates and scatter with the remaining chopped mint. Turn out the timbales – they will come out easily – arrange one on each plate and top with a Parmesan crisp.

Stir-fry with sizzling tofu

PREPARATION 15 MINUTES, PLUS MARINATING COOKING 15 MINUTES SERVES 6

1 TABLESPOON SESAME OIL • 2 TEASPOONS THAI RED CURRY PASTE • 2 GARLIC CLOVES, CRUSHED •

2 TEASPOONS GRATED FRESH ROOT GINGER • 300g (10oz) BEAN SPROUTS • 1 RED PEPPER, CORED,

DESEEDED AND THINLY SLICED • BUNCH OF SPRING ONIONS, TRIMMED AND CHOPPED • 125g (4oz)

BUTTON MUSHROOMS • 150g (5oz) MANGETOUT, HALVED LENGTHWAYS • 1 TABLESPOON SOY SAUCE •

CORIANDER LEAVES, TO GARNISH

TOFU 1 TABLESPOON GRATED FRESH ROOT GINGER • 4 GARLIC CLOVES, CRUSHED • 1 TEASPOON BROWN

SUGAR • 1 TEASPOON DIJON MUSTARD • 4 TABLESPOONS SOY SAUCE • 500g (1lb) FIRM TOFU, CUT INTO

5mm (¼ inch) SLICES • VERY LIGHT OLIVE OIL FOR SHALLOW-FRYING

1 Start with the tofu. Put the ginger, garlic, sugar, mustard and soy sauce in a shallow dish and mix together. Toss the pieces of tofu in this mixture until they are well coated. Leave to marinate for as long as you can – 10–30 minutes or up to 24 hours.

2 To make the stir-fry, heat the sesame oil in a wok until smoking hot. Add the curry paste and stir for a few seconds over the heat, then add the garlic and ginger, and stir again. Add all the vegetables to the wok and stir-fry for 1–2 minutes, then cover and leave to cook for 5 minutes or until the vegetables are tender. Stir in the soy sauce.

3 Meanwhile, drain the tofu, saving any remaining marinade. Fry the tofu on both sides in a little hot olive oil. You will probably have to do this in two batches so keep the finished pieces hot under a preheated grill.

4 Add any reserved marinade to the vegetables. Check the seasoning and add some salt if necessary, then serve with the sizzling hot tofu and garnish with coriander.

A fine microplane grater revolutionizes garlic crushing; just grate the garlic, skin and all, for perfect results. (It also works for fresh root ginger – there is no need to peel it first.) Immerse the grater in water immediately after use to make cleaning easier.

Almond and lemon cake with Moroccan orange salad

PREPARATION 30 MINUTES COOKING 30–35 MINUTES SERVES 6

75g (3oz) BUTTER, SOFTENED • 2 TABLESPOONS OLIVE OIL • 125g (4oz) CASTER SUGAR • 3 EGGS •

FINELY GRATED RIND OF 2 LEMONS • 200g (7oz) GROUND ALMONDS • ½ TEASPOON BAKING POWDER •

2–3 TABLESPOONS LIMONE LIQUEUR (OPTIONAL)

ORANGE SALAD 8 JUICY ORANGES • 2–3 TABLESPOONS CLEAR HONEY • 2–3 TEASPOONS ORANGE FLOWER

WATER • WHIPPED CREAM, TO SERVE (OPTIONAL)

1 Line a 15–18cm (6–7 inch) cake tin with nonstick baking paper.

2 Whisk together the butter, olive oil and caster sugar, until light and creamy. Add the eggs and lemon rind and whisk again until light and fluffy, then stir in the ground almonds and baking powder until thoroughly combined. Spoon the mixture into the prepared cake tin and gently level the top.

3 Bake in a preheated oven, 160°C (325°F), Gas Mark 3, for 30–35 minutes, until risen and firm to a light touch and a skewer inserted into the centre comes out clean. Cool on a wire rack. When the cake is cold, remove the paper and brush the top generously with the lemon liqueur, if using, allowing it to soak into the cake.

4 To make the orange salad, hold the oranges over a bowl to catch the juice, cut off the peel and white pith, then cut out the segments, letting them fall into the bowl, leaving behind the white inner skin. Stir in the honey and orange flower water to taste, then chill. Taste again before serving and add more honey and orange flower water if necessary.

5 Serve the cake with the orange salad and a bowl of whipped cream if liked.

White chocolate ice cream with summer berry sauce

PREPARATION 30 MINUTES, PLUS COOLING AND FREEZING COOKING 10 MINUTES SERVES 6

2 EGGS • 275ml (9fl oz) SINGLE CREAM • 75g (3oz) CASTER SUGAR • 300g (10oz) WHITE CHOCOLATE, BROKEN INTO PIECES • 275ml (9fl oz) DOUBLE CREAM

SAUCE 1kg (2lb) MIXED SUMMER BERRIES, SUCH AS REDCURRANTS, BLACKCURRANTS, BLUEBERRIES, RASPBERRIES AND BLACKBERRIES • 50–125g (2–4oz) CASTER SUGAR

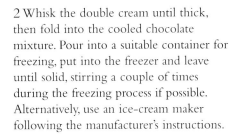

1 To make the ice cream, whisk the eggs in a bowl. Pour the single cream into a saucepan, bring to the boil and pour over the eggs. Whisk, then pour the mixture back into the saucepan. Cook over a very gentle heat, stirring all the time, for a few minutes, until the mixture coats the back of the spoon very lightly. Remove from the heat and stir in the white chocolate. Cover and set aside, stirring from time to time to help the chocolate melt.

2 Whisk the double cream until thick, then fold into the cooled chocolate mixture. Pour into a suitable container for freezing, put into the freezer and leave until solid, stirring a couple of times during the freezing process if possible. Alternatively, use an ice-cream maker following the manufacturer's instructions.

3 To make the sauce, put the fruit and caster sugar into a saucepan and heat gently until the juices run – this will take only a few minutes. Remove from the heat, taste and add more caster sugar to taste if necessary, remembering that the ice cream is quite sweet, so a sharpness in the sauce makes a pleasant contrast.

4 To serve, remove the ice cream from the freezer about 30 minutes in advance so that it can soften slightly, then serve in scoops with the sauce.

Little lemon cheesecakes with blueberries

PREPARATION 25 MINUTES SERVES 6

175g (6oz) GINGER BISCUITS • 75g (3oz) BUTTER, MELTED • 175g (6oz) BLUEBERRIES • ICING SUGAR
FOR SPRINKLING

TOPPING 400g (13oz) LOW-FAT SOFT CREAM CHEESE • FINELY GRATED RIND OF 2 LEMONS •
25g (1oz) CASTER SUGAR • 150ml (¼ pint) DOUBLE CREAM • 4 TABLESPOONS FRESHLY SQUEEZED LEMON JUICE

1 Put the biscuits into a polythene bag, close the top, then crush with a rolling pin. Tip the crushed biscuits into a bowl, add the melted butter and mix to combine. Divide the mixture between 6 x 9–10cm (3½–4 inch) loose-bottomed flan tins, pressing it on to the base in an even layer (don't attempt to go up the sides). Place in the freezer or refrigerator while you prepare the topping.

2 If there is any liquid on top of the cream cheese, pour it away, then put the cheese into a bowl and add the lemon rind and caster sugar. Stir to make a creamy mixture, then add the double cream and whisk until thick. Add the lemon juice and stir with a spoon – the acid in the juice will make the mixture even thicker.

3 Spoon the cream cheese mixture into the flan tins. Take the mixture to the edges, but don't try to smooth the surface. Refrigerate until required.

4 To finish, lift the little cheesecakes out of the tins – they will come out easily – and gently slide them on to individual plates, removing the bases of the tins as you do so. Decorate the tops with blueberries, dust with icing sugar and serve as soon as possible.

CLASSICS WITH A TWIST

People often ask how I come up with new ideas. The answer is that I get bored easily and I want to try new flavours. I'll experiment with something until I've got it right, then I'll try something new. My husband once said that he gets to eat a specific dish at every meal while I'm perfecting it, then the recipe goes into a book and he never tastes it again!

I really enjoyed working on this chapter, playing around with colours, flavours and textures and giving a new twist to old favourites. I hope you'll enjoy the results as much as I did when I was developing them.

No-rice nori sushi

PREPARATION 20 MINUTES MAKES 16–20

750g (1½lb) DAIKON OR TURNIPS, PEELED AND GRATED • 2 TEASPOONS RICE VINEGAR OR WINE VINEGAR •
2 TEASPOONS SUGAR • 4–5 PIECES OF NORI SEAWEED • I RED PEPPER, CORED, DESEEDED AND CUT INTO
LONG STRIPS • ½ CUCUMBER, PEELED AND CUT INTO LONG STRIPS • I AVOCADO, PEELED, HALVED, STONED
AND CUT INTO LONG STRIPS • SALT AND PEPPER • TOASTED SESAME SEEDS, TO GARNISH (OPTIONAL) •
SOY SAUCE DIP (SEE PAGE 150), WASABI PASTE AND PICKLED GINGER, TO SERVE

1 Squeeze the grated daikon or turnip with your hands to extract as much moisture as possible (you need a fairly dry mixture). Mix in the vinegar and sugar and add salt and pepper to taste.

2 Place a piece of nori, shiny side down, on a board and cover it lightly with the daikon or turnip mixture, leaving a 1cm (½ inch) gap at the end farthest from you. Squeeze out any extra liquid, as necessary.

3 Put a row of red pepper strips on top, at the end closest to you, about 2.5cm (1 inch) from the edge. Place a thin line of cucumber and one of avocado next to the red pepper. Fold over the end closest to you, quite firmly, then continue to roll the nori up, like a Swiss roll. Continue in the same way until all the ingredients have been used. Refrigerate until required.

4 To serve, trim the two ends of each roll – these tend to be a little untidy – then cut the rolls into 4 pieces and put them, filling-side up, on a serving plate. Sprinkle with a few sesame seeds, if liked. Serve with the soy sauce dip, a little bowl of wasabi paste and some pickled ginger.

Fruity guacamole

PREPARATION 25 MINUTES SERVES 4

I LARGE GARLIC CLOVE • I GREEN CHILLI, DESEEDED • I BUNCH OF CORIANDER, STALKS REMOVED •
JUICE AND PARED OR GRATED RIND OF I LIME • 2 RIPE AVOCADOS, PEELED, STONED AND ROUGHLY CHOPPED •
I POMEGRANATE • I RIPE PEACH, PEELED, STONED AND CHOPPED • SALT • 2 LITTLE GEM LETTUCES,
LEAVES SEPARATED AND HEARTS QUARTERED, TO SERVE

1 Put the garlic and chilli into a food processor with most of the coriander, saving a few coriander leaves for garnishing. Whiz until finely chopped. Add the lime rind and juice (perhaps holding back a few strands of rind to garnish), the avocado and a little salt and whiz to a green cream. Transfer to a mixing bowl.

2 Cut the pomegranate in half and bend back the skin – as if you were turning it inside out – to make the ruby jewelled fruits pop out. Gently fold most of the pomegranate fruit and the chopped peach into the avocado mixture.

3 Arrange the lettuce leaves and hearts around the edge of a serving dish. Heap the guacamole on top, then lightly stud it with the remaining peach and pomegranate and scatter over the reserved coriander leaves and lime rind. Serve as soon as possible.

An authentic Mexican twist on an old favourite – a wonderful taste explosion of hot and salty, sweet and sour. It makes a wonderful starter, but you must prepare it just before serving for the best colour.

Red pepper hummus with smoked paprika

PREPARATION 15 MINUTES SERVES 4

2 GARLIC CLOVES • 410g (13½oz) CAN CHICKPEAS, DRAINED • ½ X 325g (11oz) JAR WHOLE SWEET RED PEPPERS, DRAINED • 1 TEASPOON HONEY • TABASCO, TO TASTE • ¼–½ TEASPOON SMOKED PAPRIKA • COARSELY GROUND BLACK PEPPER • WARM OR GRIDDLED PITTA BREAD, TO SERVE

1 Whiz the garlic cloves in a food processor until chopped, then add the chickpeas, red peppers and honey and whiz again. Stir in the Tabasco and smoked paprika to taste.

2 Turn the mixture on to a flat plate and smooth the surface. Grind some black pepper coarsely over the top and serve with strips of warm or griddled pitta bread.

Using sweet peppers from a jar makes this recipe very quick and easy. Smoked paprika gives an intriguing, unusual flavour, but if you can't find it use mild paprika instead.

Warm purple-sprouting broccoli caesar with toasted almonds

PREPARATION 15 MINUTES COOKING 4–5 MINUTES SERVES 4

250g (8oz) TRIMMED PURPLE-SPROUTING BROCCOLI • 1 COS LETTUCE, OUTER LEAVES REMOVED,

OR 2 LETTUCE HEARTS

DRESSING 4 TABLESPOONS MAYONNAISE • 1 TABLESPOON LEMON JUICE • TABASCO SAUCE, TO TASTE •

6 TABLESPOONS PARMESAN CHEESE SHAVINGS • 2 TABLESPOONS TOASTED FLAKED ALMONDS • SALT AND PEPPER

1 Cook the broccoli in a saucepan of boiling water for 4–5 minutes or until just tender – the time will depend on the thickness of the stems. Drain.

2 Meanwhile, make the dressing by mixing together the mayonnaise, lemon juice and enough Tabasco to give it a good zing. Season with salt and pepper and stir in half the Parmesan.

3 Tear the lettuce into pieces and put into a bowl with the broccoli. Pour the dressing over and toss lightly. Top with the remaining Parmesan and the almonds and serve immediately.

Use a home-made lemon mayonnaise (see page 143) or a good-quality bought one as the basis of the dressing. I pep up the flavour with Tabasco instead of Worcestershire sauce, which contains anchovy essence.

Oven-baked ratatouille with balsamic vinegar and caper berries

PREPARATION 10 MINUTES COOKING 40 MINUTES SERVES 4

2 PURPLE ONIONS, EACH SLICED INTO 6 OR 8 • 1 LARGE COURGETTE, CUT INTO 1cm (½ inch) PIECES • 1 LARGE AUBERGINE, CUT INTO 1cm (½ inch) PIECES • 2 RED PEPPERS, CORED, DESEEDED AND CUT INTO 1cm (½ inch) PIECES • 2 TABLESPOONS OLIVE OIL • 1–2 TABLESPOONS BALSAMIC VINEGAR • 400g (13oz) CAN CHOPPED TOMATOES • 4 GARLIC CLOVES, ROUGHLY CHOPPED • 1–2 TABLESPOONS CAPER BERRIES, DRAINED • SALT AND PEPPER

1 Put the onions, courgette, aubergine and peppers into a roasting tin with the olive oil and 1 tablespoon of the balsamic vinegar. Toss the vegetables to coat them all with the oil and vinegar, then season with salt and pepper.

2 Bake in a preheated oven, 200°C (400°F), Gas Mark 6, uncovered, for 20 minutes, then add the tomatoes, garlic and caper berries. Stir well and cook for another 20 minutes, or until all the vegetables are tender.

3 Taste the ratatouille and add a little more balsamic vinegar and salt and pepper, if necessary. Serve hot, warm or cold.

Thai-flavoured mushroom stroganoff with golden rice

PREPARATION 15 MINUTES COOKING 15 MINUTES SERVES 4

1 TABLESPOON RAPESEED OIL • 500g (1lb) BABY MUSHROOMS, HALVED OR QUARTERED DEPENDING ON SIZE •
2 LEMON GRASS STALKS, CRUSHED • 4–6 LIME LEAVES OR THE GRATED RIND OF 1 LIME • 1 TABLESPOON
GRATED FRESH ROOT GINGER • 4 TEASPOONS CORNFLOUR • 2 X 400ml (14fl oz) CANS COCONUT MILK •
SALT AND PEPPER • 4 TABLESPOONS ROUGHLY CHOPPED CORIANDER LEAVES, TO GARNISH
RICE 300g (10oz) WHITE BASMATI RICE • PINCH OF TURMERIC • 600ml (1 pint) WATER

1 Start with the rice. Put it into a heavy-based saucepan with the turmeric, a little salt if you like, and the water. Bring to the boil, then cover, turn the heat right down and leave to cook very gently for 15 minutes, or until the water has been absorbed and the rice is tender. Fluff with a fork and keep warm, covered, until required.

2 Meanwhile, heat the rapeseed oil in a large saucepan, add the mushrooms, stir, cover and cook for about 5 minutes, or until tender.

3 Add the lemon grass, lime leaves or rind and ginger and stir over the heat for a few seconds to release the flavours.

4 Blend the cornflour to a thin paste with a little of the coconut milk and set aside. Add the remaining coconut milk to the mushrooms, bring to the boil and simmer for 5 minutes, then pour in the cornflour paste, bring to the boil and stir for a minute or so as it thickens. Season with salt and pepper, then remove the lemon grass (and, if you like, the lime leaves, if using).

5 Serve the stroganoff with the hot cooked rice topped with the coriander.

For a lighter version, use half coconut milk and half water, which is better value than buying 'light' coconut milk where you're simply paying for the water – read the ingredients on the label!

Lentil shepherd's pie with smoky cheese mash

PREPARATION 30 MINUTES COOKING 1 HOUR SERVES 4

1.1kg (2¼lb) POTATOES, PEELED AND CUT INTO EVEN-SIZED PIECES • 2 TABLESPOONS OLIVE OIL • 2 LARGE ONIONS, CHOPPED • 2 GARLIC CLOVES, CRUSHED • 400g (13oz) CAN CHOPPED TOMATOES • 410g (13½oz) CAN GREEN LENTILS, DRAINED • 50g (2oz) SUN-BLUSH TOMATOES, CHOPPED • 1 TABLESPOON TOMATO KETCHUP • 15g (½oz) BUTTER • 200g (7oz) SMOKED WENSLEYDALE OR CHEDDAR CHEESE, GRATED OR CRUMBLED • SALT AND PEPPER • COOKED PETIT POIS OR KALE, TO SERVE

1 Put the potatoes in a saucepan, cover with water and bring to the boil. Boil for about 20 minutes, or until tender.

2 Meanwhile, heat the olive oil in a large saucepan. Add the chopped onions, cover and fry for 15 minutes, or until very tender, lightly browned and sweet. Remove from the heat and add the garlic, chopped tomatoes, lentils, sun-blush tomatoes and tomato ketchup. Season with salt and pepper to taste.

3 Drain the boiled potatoes, reserving the water, then mash with the butter and enough of the reserved water to make a creamy consistency. Stir in two-thirds of the cheese.

4 Pour the lentil mixture into a shallow casserole dish and spread the potato on top. Scatter with the remaining cheese and bake in a preheated oven, 200°C (400°F), Gas Mark 6, for 40 minutes, until golden brown. Serve with petit pois or kale.

This is such a tasty, satisfying dish and I find it goes down very well with even the most hardened carnivores. It's convenient, too, because it can be made in advance, ready for the final cooking.

Three-bean chilli with multi-coloured peppers

PREPARATION 20 MINUTES COOKING 30–35 MINUTES SERVES 4

I TABLESPOON OLIVE OIL • I ONION, CHOPPED • 2 GARLIC CLOVES, FINELY CHOPPED • I GREEN CHILLI,

DESEEDED AND CHOPPED • I RED, I YELLOW AND I GREEN PEPPER, ALL CORED, DESEEDED AND CHOPPED •

410g (13½oz) CAN BORLOTTI BEANS • 410g (13½oz) CAN RED KIDNEY BEANS • 410g (13½oz) CAN PINTO BEANS

• 400g (13oz) CAN CHOPPED TOMATOES • SALT AND PEPPER • TABASCO SAUCE (OPTIONAL)

1 Heat the olive oil in a large saucepan, add the onion, cover and fry without browning for 5 minutes. Add the garlic, chilli and peppers, stir, then cover and fry for a further 15–20 minutes, or until the peppers are tender.

2 Add all the beans, together with their liquid, and the tomatoes. Stir and bring to a simmer, then cook over a gentle heat for about 10 minutes, until the vegetables are very tender.

3 Taste and season with salt and pepper as necessary, and a dash of Tabasco sauce if you think it needs to be a bit hotter, then serve.

Kedgeree with eggs and tarragon butter

PREPARATION 20 MINUTES COOKING 35 MINUTES SERVES 4

I TABLESPOON OLIVE OIL • I LARGE ONION, CHOPPED • 3 GARLIC CLOVES, FINELY CHOPPED •

¼ TEASPOON TURMERIC • 300g (10oz) BASMATI RICE • 150g (5oz) SPLIT RED LENTILS • 750ml (1¼ pints) WATER

• 2 TABLESPOONS LEMON JUICE • 4–6 HENS' EGGS OR 8–12 QUAILS' EGGS, HARD-BOILED AND HALVED

• SALT AND PEPPER

TARRAGON BUTTER 75g (3oz) BUTTER, SOFTENED • 4 TABLESPOONS CHOPPED TARRAGON

1 Heat the olive oil in a large, heavy-based saucepan, add the onion, cover and cook gently for 10 minutes, stirring from time to time.

2 Stir in the garlic and turmeric and cook for a minute or two longer, then add the rice and lentils and stir until they are coated with the onion and spice mixture.

3 Pour in the water, bring to the boil, then cover and leave to cook very gently for 20 minutes, when the lentils will be pale, the rice tender and all the water absorbed.

4 While the rice is cooking, make the tarragon butter. Beat the butter with a fork until creamy, then stir in the tarragon. Form into a sausage shape on a piece of greaseproof paper or foil and refrigerate until required.

5 Using a fork, gently stir the lemon juice into the rice – this will brighten the colour instantly – and season with salt and pepper. Turn the mixture into a shallow warmed serving dish or on to individual plates and top with pieces of tarragon butter and the cooked eggs.

Tamari-flavoured nut roast with tomato sauce

PREPARATION 40 MINUTES COOKING 1½ HOURS SERVES 4

1 TABLESPOON OLIVE OIL • 1 LARGE ONION, CHOPPED • 4 GARLIC CLOVES, FINELY CHOPPED •

2 X 400g (13oz) CANS CHOPPED TOMATOES • 20g (¾oz) BASIL • 125g (4oz) MUSHROOMS, CHOPPED •

125g (4oz) WHOLEMEAL BREADCRUMBS • 125g (4oz) PECAN NUTS, CHOPPED • 125g (4oz) GROUND ALMONDS •

1 TABLESPOON TAMARI • ½ TEASPOON YEAST EXTRACT • 1 EGG • SALT AND PEPPER

1 Heat the olive oil in a large, heavy-based saucepan, add the onion, cover and cook gently for 10 minutes, stirring from time to time. Stir in the garlic and cook for a minute or two longer, then add the tomatoes. Cook, uncovered, for about 20 minutes, or until the liquid has disappeared and the mixture is very thick.

2 Meanwhile, remove one good sprig of basil for garnishing and set aside; roughly chop the rest.

3 Tip half the tomato mixture into a large bowl and add the chopped basil, mushrooms, breadcrumbs, pecan nuts, almonds, tamari, yeast extract and egg. Mix well and season with salt and pepper.

4 Line the base and wide sides of a 500g (1lb) loaf tin with a strip of nonstick baking paper. Spoon the mixture into the tin, smooth the top and cover lightly with another piece of nonstick baking paper. Bake in a preheated oven, 180°C (350°F), Gas Mark 4, for 1 hour.

5 Let the nut roast stand for 3–4 minutes to settle while you reheat the remaining tomato mixture and season it with salt and pepper. You could thin it with a little water for a pouring consistency if you wish, or leave it chunky.

6 Slip a knife around the edges of the nut roast, turn it out and strip off the paper. Garnish with the reserved basil sprig and serve in thick slices, accompanied by the tomato sauce.

Start this recipe by making the tomato sauce: use some of it in the nut roast mixture and serve the rest of the sauce with the cooked nut roast.

Courgette, ricotta and petit pois lasagne

PREPARATION 30 MINUTES COOKING I HOUR SERVES 4

ABOUT 9 SHEETS OF READY-TO-USE LASAGNE • I TABLESPOON OLIVE OIL • 2 ONIONS, CHOPPED •
500g (1lb) COURGETTES, THINLY SLICED • 275g (9oz) FROZEN PETIT POIS • 4 TABLESPOONS CHOPPED MINT •
500g (1lb) RICOTTA CHEESE • 300ml (½ pint) MILK • 300ml (½ pint) SOURED CREAM • 75g (3oz) PARMESAN
CHEESE, FRESHLY GRATED • SALT AND PEPPER • CRUNCHY GREEN SALAD, TO SERVE

1 Put the lasagne into a bowl or shallow dish, cover with cold water and leave to soak while you prepare the filling. This presoaking makes ready-to-use lasagne so much lighter and nicer.

2 Heat the olive oil in a large saucepan, add the onions and fry gently for 5 minutes, until beginning to soften, then add the courgettes. Cover and cook gently for 15–20 minutes, or until the vegetables are tender but not browned. Stir in the petit pois and mint, season with salt and pepper and remove from the heat.

3 Mix the ricotta with 2 tablespoons of the milk, to soften it a little, and season with black pepper.

4 Drain the lasagne and arrange a single layer in the base of your casserole. Spread half the ricotta over the lasagne and put half of the courgette mixture over that. Top with another layer of lasagne, then the remaining ricotta and the courgette mixture. Finish with a layer of lasagne.

5 To make the topping, spoon the soured cream into a bowl and gradually stir in the remaining milk. Pour this mixture over the top of the lasagne, then sprinkle thickly with the Parmesan. Bake in a preheated oven, 200°C (400°F), Gas Mark 6, for 40 minutes, until puffy, golden brown and smelling gorgeous. I like to serve it with a crunchy green salad.

The dish I use is a shallow one that will take three sheets of lasagne in a row across the base – you may need to adjust the amount of lasagne to the size of your dish.

Whiskey cream banoffi

PREPARATION 20 MINUTES, PLUS CHILLING COOKING 3–4 HOURS SERVES 4–6

400g (13oz) CAN CONDENSED MILK • 250g (8oz) DIGESTIVE BISCUITS • 125g (4oz) BUTTER, MELTED •

2–3 LARGE BANANAS • 300ml (½ pint) DOUBLE CREAM • 4 TABLESPOONS BAILEY'S CREAM LIQUEUR •

25g (1oz) DARK CHOCOLATE, GRATED

1 Put the unopened can of condensed milk into a deep saucepan and add cold water to cover it by at least 5cm (2 inches) – you can put the tin on its side if it fits better. Bring to the boil and let it simmer for 3–4 hours. Make sure you keep the water level topped up so that it's always at least 5cm (2 inches) above the can (set a timer to remind you). This process is perfectly safe as long as you follow these instructions. Allow the can to cool in the water.

2 Put the biscuits in a large polythene bag, close the top, then crush with a rolling pin to make fine crumbs. Mix the biscuit crumbs with the melted butter, then press into the base of a 20–23cm (8–9 inch) flan dish. If there's time, put this into the refrigerator for 10–15 minutes to chill.

3 Peel the bananas and slice each in half lengthways. Lay the slices of banana, cut-side down, in the flan case, cutting them as necessary to make them fit.

4 Spoon the caramelized condensed milk evenly over the bananas, to cover them.

5 Whip the double cream with the Bailey's until it stands in soft peaks, then spoon on top of the caramel, taking it to the edges of the dish. Sprinkle grated chocolate all over the top. Chill until required – if anything, this tastes even better after 24 hours.

To make the toffee layer you need to caramelize the condensed milk. You can caramelize more than one can at a time as long as they are all covered with water as described above. They will keep for months, enabling you to make this yummy pudding quickly.

Chilled rosewater rice pudding

PREPARATION 10 MINUTES, PLUS COOLING COOKING 45 MINUTES SERVES 4

125g (4oz) PUDDING RICE • 900ml (1½ pints) MILK OR SOYA MILK • 125g (4oz) CASTER OR LIGHT BROWN SUGAR • GRATED RIND OF 1 LEMON • 2 TABLESPOONS ROSEWATER • 300ml (½ pint) DOUBLE CREAM, LIGHTLY WHIPPED (OPTIONAL)

TO DECORATE THIN STRIPS OF LEMON RIND • 25g (1oz) FLAKED ALMONDS, TOASTED • A FEW FRAGRANT RED ROSE PETALS (OPTIONAL)

1 Put the rice into a saucepan with plenty of water, bring to the boil and simmer for about 15 minutes, or until it is beginning to soften, but still hard in the centre.

2 Drain the rice and return to the pan with the milk or soya milk, caster or light brown sugar and grated lemon rind. Bring to the boil, cover and simmer for about 30 minutes, stirring from time to time, more frequently towards the end, or until the rice is tender and the consistency quite thick and creamy. Allow to cool completely.

3 Stir the rosewater into the pudding, then fold in the whipped cream, if using. Spoon the mixture into a shallow serving dish or individual bowls. Just before serving, scatter with the pared lemon rind, almonds and rose petals, if you have them.

NO TIME TO COOK

Nothing can beat the satisfaction of cooking your own food and the joy of using health-giving ingredients. Then there are the delicious aromas, the tasting and getting a dish just right and watching the pleasure it gives to others. There's nothing more welcoming than a home fragrant with warm cooking smells. Home-cooked food nourishes the soul as well as the body.

But I am a realist. I know time and energy are precious, especially during the working week. So here are recipes that taste good, yet can be made when you have limited time to cook.

Soft polenta with leeks and dolcelatte

PREPARATION 15 MINUTES COOKING 20 MINUTES SERVES 4

500g (1lb) TRIMMED LEEKS, SLICED INTO 5cm (2 inch) LENGTHS • 250g (8oz) DRY POLENTA •

250g (8oz) DOLCELATTE CHEESE, BROKEN INTO PIECES • SALT AND PEPPER • GOOD-QUALITY OLIVE OIL

(OPTIONAL) AND COARSELY GROUND BLACK PEPPER, TO GARNISH

1 Add the leeks to a saucepan half-filled with boiling water. Cover and cook for 8–10 minutes, or until the leeks are very tender. Drain, reserving the water, and keep the leeks warm.

2 Measure the cooking water and make up to 900ml (1½ pints) with more water, if necessary. Put this liquid into a large saucepan and heat to a boil. Sprinkle the polenta on top in a steady stream, stirring all the time with a wooden spoon. Cook for 1–2 minutes, until thick and soft, then remove from the heat.

3 Add the leeks, dolcelatte and a seasoning of salt and pepper (remembering that the cheese is very salty) to the polenta and stir gently to distribute the leeks and cheese through the mixture. Serve on to warmed plates, swirl with a little olive oil if using, and grind some coarse black pepper over the top.

Crisp-fried tempeh with onion gravy

PREPARATION 20 MINUTES COOKING 30 MINUTES SERVES 4

2 X 200g (7oz) BLOCKS OF TEMPEH • LIGHT OLIVE OIL OR RAPESEED OIL FOR SHALLOW-FRYING •

2–4 TABLESPOONS SOY SAUCE • COOKED KALE OR CABBAGE, TO SERVE

GRAVY 2 TABLESPOONS OLIVE OIL • 2 ONIONS, SLICED • 2 GARLIC CLOVES, CRUSHED • I TABLESPOON

CORNFLOUR OR ARROWROOT • 450ml (¾ pint) VEGETABLE STOCK • I TABLESPOON SOY SAUCE • SALT

AND PEPPER

1 To make the gravy, heat the olive oil in a large saucepan, add the onions, cover and cook over a gentle heat for 15–20 minutes, or until very soft and lightly browned. If necessary, turn up the heat and stir the onions for a minute or two until nut brown in colour.

2 Add the garlic and cook for a minute or two, then stir the cornflour or arrowroot into the onions. Gradually pour in the vegetable stock, stirring all the time, and simmer for 2–3 minutes, until thick. Remove from the heat and add the soy sauce and salt and pepper to taste. Set aside ready to reheat just before serving.

3 Cut the tempeh into slices about 2.5mm (⅛ inch) thick and the length of the pack, or half that. Cover the base of a frying pan lightly with olive or rapeseed oil and heat. When it sizzles immediately when a speck of tempeh is dropped into it, put in the slices in a single layer (you may have to do more than one batch) and fry for about one minute on each side, until crisp and golden brown.

4 Drain the tempeh on kitchen paper, then place on a plate, sprinkle with soy sauce, and serve with the gravy and kale or cabbage.

Sesame-roasted tofu with satay sauce and broccoli

PREPARATION 20 MINUTES COOKING 20 MINUTES SERVES 4

500g (1lb) TOFU, DRAINED • 4 TABLESPOONS SOY SAUCE • 2 TABLESPOONS ROASTED SESAME OIL •
2 TABLESPOONS SESAME SEEDS • 2 HEADS OF BROCCOLI, ABOUT 350g (11½oz) EACH, TRIMMED AND BROKEN
INTO FLORETS
SATAY SAUCE 4 HEAPED TABLESPOONS PEANUT BUTTER (PLAIN OR CRUNCHY) • 400ml (14fl oz) CAN
COCONUT MILK (SEE PAGE 41) • 2 GARLIC CLOVES, CRUSHED • 2 TEASPOONS GRATED FRESH ROOT GINGER •
¼–½ TEASPOON DRIED RED CHILLI FLAKES • 2–3 TEASPOONS BROWN SUGAR • 4 TABLESPOONS CHOPPED
CORIANDER, TO GARNISH

1 Blot the tofu dry on kitchen paper and cut into thin strips about 5mm (¼ inch) thick. Put the strips on a plate in a single layer, pour the soy sauce on top, then turn the strips so that they are all coated.

2 Heat the sesame oil in a grill pan or shallow roasting tin under a preheated hot grill. Put the tofu strips in the pan or tin in a single layer and scatter with half the sesame seeds, then immediately turn them over and coat with the remaining sesame seeds.

3 Put the pan or tin back under the heat and grill for about 10 minutes, or until the tofu is crisp and browned, then turn the pieces over and grill the other side.

4 Meanwhile, make the satay sauce. Put the peanut butter into a saucepan and gradually stir in the coconut milk to make a smooth sauce, then add the garlic, ginger and chilli. Heat gently, taste and add sugar to taste. Remove from the heat and set aside until required.

5 About 5–10 minutes before the tofu is ready, heat 1cm (½ inch) depth of water in a large saucepan and bring to the boil. Add the broccoli, cover and cook for 4–5 minutes, or until just tender. Drain.

6 Put some broccoli, tofu and a serving of satay sauce on each plate, scatter the sauce with some coriander, and serve.

Laksa

PREPARATION 15 MINUTES COOKING 20 MINUTES SERVES 4

125g (4oz) RICE NOODLES • 2 TABLESPOONS OIL • 1 TABLESPOON VEGETARIAN THAI PASTE •

250g (8oz) SHIITAKE MUSHROOMS, SLICED • 1 RED CHILLI, DESEEDED AND SLICED • 400ml (14fl oz) CAN

COCONUT MILK (SEE PAGE 41) • 600ml (1 pint) WATER • 1 AUBERGINE • 2 PAK CHOI, TRIMMED AND HALVED •

125g (4oz) BABY SWEETCORN, HALVED DIAGONALLY • SALT AND PEPPER • 20g (¾oz) CORIANDER, ROUGHLY

CHOPPED, TO GARNISH

1 Put the noodles into a bowl and cover with boiling water. Soak for 5–10 minutes, then drain.

2 Heat 1 tablespoon of the oil in a large saucepan, add the Thai paste and let it sizzle for a few seconds until aromatic, then stir in the mushrooms and chilli. Pour in the coconut milk and water, reduce the heat, cover and leave to simmer for 10–15 minutes.

3 Meanwhile, cut the aubergine into 7mm (⅓ inch) slices and brush on both sides with the remaining oil. Place in a grill pan and cook under a preheated grill until tender and lightly browned – about 7 minutes on each side. Set aside to cool, then cut into dice.

4 Cook the pak choi in boiling water for about 6 minutes, or until tender; drain well.

5 Add the noodles, aubergine, pak choi and sweetcorn to the coconut mixture. Bring to the boil and simmer gently for a minute or two, to heat everything through and cook the sweetcorn.

6 Season with salt and pepper as necessary, ladle into warmed bowls and top each with some coriander to garnish.

You need Thai paste for this Malaysian soup/stew – most contain shrimp paste so read the label to find one that's vegetarian.

Banana curry with cashew rice

PREPARATION 25 MINUTES COOKING 30 MINUTES SERVES 4

500g (1lb) BABY POTATOES, HALVED • 2 TABLESPOONS OLIVE OIL • 1 ONION, CHOPPED • 2 GREEN
PEPPERS, CORED, DESEEDED AND CHOPPED • 2 TEASPOONS MUSTARD SEEDS • ½ TEASPOON TURMERIC •
1 TABLESPOON GRATED FRESH ROOT GINGER • 4 GARLIC CLOVES, CRUSHED • 5g (¼oz) OR SMALL BUNCH
OF CURRY LEAVES • 4 LARGE, UNDER-RIPE BANANAS, SLICED • 300ml (½ pint) WATER • 75g (3oz) CREAMED
COCONUT, CUT INTO PIECES • 4 TEASPOONS FRESH, SIEVED AND DESEEDED TAMARIND (FROM A JAR) •
SALT AND PEPPER

RICE 300g (10oz) BASMATI RICE • 125g (4oz) ROASTED CASHEW NUTS, CHOPPED

1 Start by cooking the rice. Bring a large saucepan of water to the boil, add the rice, bring back to the boil, then leave to simmer for 15–20 minutes, or until the rice is just tender. Drain in a colander, rinse with boiling water, drain again well, then return it to the saucepan and keep it warm over a gentle heat until needed.

2 To make the curry, put the potatoes into a saucepan, cover with water, bring to the boil and simmer for 10–15 minutes until just tender, then drain.

3 Meanwhile, heat the olive oil in a large, heavy-based saucepan, add the onion and peppers, cover and cook gently for 10 minutes, stirring from time to time.

4 Add the mustard seeds, stirring over the heat for a minute or two until they start to pop, then stir in the turmeric, ginger, garlic and curry leaves and cook for a minute or two longer.

5 Stir in the drained potatoes and the bananas, then add the water, coconut and tamarind paste. Bring to the boil, then leave to cook gently for 5–10 minutes, until the sauce is thick and the flavours blended. Season with salt and pepper.

6 Quickly add the cashews to the rice and fork through, then serve the rice and curry together on warmed plates.

I love this gentle, sweet curry and it's so quick to make. You could use 2–3 plantains in place of the bananas if you prefer but cook them for a few minutes longer.

Tagliatelle with creamy spinach and nutmeg sauce

PREPARATION 15 MINUTES COOKING 20 MINUTES SERVES 4

500g (1lb) TAGLIATELLE • 500g (1lb) READY-TO-COOK SPINACH LEAVES • 25g (1oz) BUTTER • 2 TABLESPOONS OLIVE OIL • 1 ONION, FINELY CHOPPED • 2 GARLIC CLOVES, CHOPPED • 2 TEASPOONS CORNFLOUR • 300ml (½ pint) SINGLE OR DOUBLE CREAM • FRESHLY GRATED NUTMEG • SALT AND PEPPER • GRATED PARMESAN CHEESE, TO SERVE (OPTIONAL)

1 Bring a large saucepan of water to the boil for the pasta. When it comes to the boil, add the tagliatelle and cook according to packet instructions.

2 Meanwhile, quickly rinse the spinach in cold water, then put it into a large saucepan and cook over a high heat with just the water clinging to the leaves for 3–4 minutes, or until tender. Drain thoroughly, reserving the water, and set the spinach aside. Make the water up to 150ml (¼ pint).

3 Heat the butter and 1 tablespoon of the olive oil in a large, heavy-based saucepan, add the onion, cover the pan and cook gently for 10 minutes, stirring from time to time. Stir in the garlic and cook for a minute or two longer.

4 Stir the cornflour into the saucepan, then add the spinach water and stir over the heat for a minute or two until thickened. Add the spinach and the cream, then grate in a good flavouring of nutmeg and season with salt and pepper.

5 Drain the tagliatelle and return to the pan with the remaining olive oil and toss gently. Then either add the sauce and toss with the pasta, or serve the pasta on warmed plates and spoon the spinach sauce on top. Hand round the Parmesan separately, if using.

Spaghetti with black olive and tomato sauce

PREPARATION 15 MINUTES COOKING 30 MINUTES SERVES 4

2 TABLESPOONS OLIVE OIL • 1 ONION, FINELY CHOPPED • 2 GARLIC CLOVES, CHOPPED • 2 X 400g (13oz) CANS CHOPPED TOMATOES • 250ml (8fl oz) RED WINE • 400g (13oz) SPAGHETTI • 50–125g (2–4oz) KALAMATA OLIVES, STONED AND ROUGHLY CHOPPED • SALT AND PEPPER • PARMESAN CHEESE SHAVINGS, TO SERVE (OPTIONAL)

1 Heat 1 tablespoon of the olive oil in a large, heavy-based saucepan, add the onion, cover and cook gently for 10 minutes, stirring from time to time. Stir in the garlic and cook for a minute or two longer.

2 Add the tomatoes and wine to the pan. Bring to the boil and leave to boil, uncovered, stirring from time to time, for 20 minutes or until thick.

3 Meanwhile, bring a large pan of water to the boil for the pasta. When it comes to a rolling boil, add the spaghetti and cook according to packet instructions.

4 Liquidize the sauce in a food processor or blender, or using a stick blender, and return it to the saucepan. Stir in the olives, season with salt and pepper and reheat.

5 Drain the spaghetti, return to the pan with the remaining olive oil and toss gently. Then either add the sauce and toss with the spaghetti, or serve the spaghetti on warmed plates and spoon the tomato and olive sauce on top. Hand round the Parmesan separately, if using.

Rosti with apple sauce

PREPARATION 15 MINUTES COOKING 20 MINUTES SERVES 4

1.1kg (2¼lb) BAKING POTATOES, SCRUBBED BUT NOT PEELED • 1 SMALL ONION • 1 TABLESPOON CHOPPED
ROSEMARY • 4 TABLESPOONS OLIVE OIL • SALT AND PEPPER • ROSEMARY SPRIGS, TO GARNISH
APPLE SAUCE 500g (1lb) COX APPLES, PEELED, CORED AND SLICED • 2 TABLESPOONS WATER •
CASTER SUGAR, TO TASTE

1 Grate the potatoes and onion on a medium-coarse grater, or using the grating attachment on a food processor if you have one. Mix with the rosemary and add salt and pepper to taste.

2 Heat 2 tablespoons of the olive oil in a 28cm (11 inch) frying pan. Add the potato mixture and press down firmly. Fry for 8 minutes, or until the underside is crisp and golden. Slide the rosti out on to a plate, then invert another plate on top and turn them over. Heat the remaining oil in the pan, then slide the rosti back into the pan with the cooked side uppermost, and cook for another 8 minutes.

3 While the rosti is cooking, make the apple sauce. Put the apples into a saucepan with the water, bring to the boil, cover and cook gently for 5–10 minutes, until the apples have collapsed. Mash lightly with a wooden spoon and sweeten to taste with caster sugar.

4 Turn the rosti out of the frying pan on to a large serving plate and garnish with a few rosemary sprigs. Serve in thick slices, with the apple sauce.

I love this combination: crisp, irresistible rosti with a sweet apple sauce. A salad of sliced cabbage and grated carrot tossed in vinaigrette goes well with it.

Creamy three-cheese cauliflower with walnuts

PREPARATION 15 MINUTES COOKING 20 MINUTES SERVES 4

1 CAULIFLOWER, TRIMMED AND CUT INTO 1cm (½ inch) PIECES • 300g (10oz) CREAM CHEESE • 1 TEASPOON DIJON MUSTARD • 125g (4oz) BLUE CHEESE, CRUMBLED • 25g (1oz) WALNUTS, ROUGHLY CHOPPED • 50g (2oz) CHEDDAR CHEESE, GRATED • SALT AND PEPPER • WATERCRESS SALAD, TO SERVE

1 Bring 5cm (2 inches) depth of water to the boil in a saucepan, add the cauliflower and cook for about 8 minutes, or until tender. Drain, and return the cauliflower to the pan.

2 Mix the cream cheese and mustard with the cauliflower, then stir in the blue cheese. Season with a little salt if necessary and plenty of pepper.

3 Pour the mixture into a shallow gratin dish. Scatter the walnuts on top, then cover with the Cheddar (this helps to prevent the walnuts from burning). Put under a preheated hot grill for 10–15 minutes, or until the top is golden brown and the inside hot and bubbling. Serve at once with a watercress salad.

Chargrilled artichoke heart and basil frittata

PREPARATION 10 MINUTES COOKING 15 MINUTES SERVES 4

2 X 290g (9½oz) JARS CHARGRILLED HALVED ARTICHOKE HEARTS IN OIL • 225g (7½oz) GRUYÈRE OR EMMENTAL CHEESE, GRATED • 8 EGGS, WHISKED • SALT AND PEPPER • HANDFUL OF BASIL, ROUGHLY CHOPPED

1 Drain the artichoke hearts but save the oil. Heat 2 tablespoons of the oil in a 28cm (11 inch) frying pan or in a gratin dish that will go under the grill.

2 Arrange the artichoke hearts in a single layer on the bottom of the pan or dish, sprinkle over half the cheese, then pour the eggs evenly over. Season with salt and pepper and top with the basil and the remaining cheese.

3 Set the pan over a moderate heat, cover with a lid or a plate and cook for about 5 minutes, or until the base is set and getting browned. Meanwhile preheat the grill to high.

4 Remove the covering from the pan and put the pan under the grill for about 10 minutes, or until the frittata has puffed up and browned, and is set in the centre. Serve straightaway.

If you can't get chargrilled artichoke hearts, any halved artichoke hearts in oil from a jar or loose from a deli will be fine. Any frittata that's left over is wonderful cold, perhaps served with a lemon mayonnaise and a crisp green salad.

Rocket, avocado and pine nut salad

PREPARATION 10 MINUTES SERVES 4

I TABLESPOON BALSAMIC VINEGAR • 2 TABLESPOONS OLIVE OIL • BLACK PEPPER • 8 SUN-DRIED TOMATOES, CHOPPED • 50g (2oz) RAISINS • 250g (8oz) ROCKET • 250g (8oz) PECORINO CHEESE, SHAVED OR THINLY SLICED • 25g (1oz) PINE NUTS, LIGHTLY TOASTED • I LARGE AVOCADO, PEELED, STONED AND CUT INTO CHUNKS • WARM CRUSTY BREAD, TO SERVE

1 Put the balsamic vinegar, olive oil and black pepper to taste into a large serving bowl and beat together with a spoon until combined.

2 Add the tomatoes, raisins, rocket, pecorino, pine nuts and avocado and toss everything together. Serve with warmed bread.

Some fresh, warm walnut or rye bread will make the perfect accompaniment for this summer salad.

Mascarpone, amaretti and raspberry trifles

PREPARATION 15 MINUTES SERVES 4

275g (9oz) AMARETTI BISCUITS, ROUGHLY CRUSHED • 5 TABLESPOONS AMARETTO LIQUEUR OR ORANGE JUICE •

275g (9oz) RASPBERRIES • 500g (1lb) MASCARPONE CHEESE • 25g (1oz) FLAKED ALMONDS, TOASTED

1 Put the amaretti biscuits in the bases of 4 small shallow glass bowls (or in one large glass bowl). Sprinkle the Amaretto or orange juice over the biscuits, then place the raspberries on top in an even layer.

2 Beat the mascarpone with a fork to loosen it, then spoon it on top of the raspberries and gently spread it to the edges of the bowls. Top with the toasted flaked almonds just before serving.

Mango, cardamom and pistachio fool

PREPARATION 15 MINUTES SERVES 4

½ TEASPOON CARDAMOM SEEDS • 1 LARGE, RIPE MANGO • 300ml (½ pint) DOUBLE CREAM • 2 TABLESPOONS SHELLED PISTACHIOS, HALVED

1 Crush the cardamom seeds using a pestle and mortar, or the end of a rolling pin on a board, removing the outer husks. Set aside.

2 Make two cuts through the mango straight down about 5mm (¼ inch) either side of the stalk, to cut the flesh from the flat stone. Peel off the skin and cut the flesh into rough pieces; remove as much flesh from around the stone as you can. Put all the mango flesh into a food processor, along with the cardamom, and whiz to a purée.

3 Whip the double cream until it stands in stiff peaks, then gently fold in the mango purée, not too thoroughly, to give a pretty marbled effect. Spoon the mixture into 4 glasses and top with the pistachios.

This is gorgeous, but for a less-rich version, use thick Greek yogurt, or half yogurt and half cream, whipped together.

Microwave-steamed maple syrup pudding

PREPARATION 20 MINUTES, PLUS STANDING COOKING 10 MINUTES SERVES 4

175g (6oz) BUTTER, SOFTENED • 175g (6oz) CASTER SUGAR • 6 TABLESPOONS MILK OR MILK AND WATER •
175g (6oz) SELF-RAISING FLOUR • 1½ TEASPOONS BAKING POWDER • 3 EGGS • 5 TABLESPOONS REAL MAPLE
SYRUP, PLUS EXTRA TO SERVE (OPTIONAL) • TOASTED CHOPPED WALNUTS, TO DECORATE

1 Put the butter, sugar, milk, flour, baking powder, eggs and 1 tablespoon of the maple syrup into a food processor and whiz to a creamy consistency. Alternatively, put them into a bowl and beat with a wooden spoon or hand whisk until light and fluffy.

2 Pour the remaining maple syrup into the bottom of a lightly greased plastic 1.2 litre (2 pint) microwaveable pudding bowl, then spoon the sponge mixture on top.

3 Microwave, uncovered, until the sponge has risen and a skewer inserted into the centre comes out clean. This takes about 10 minutes in my microwave, which is 650w. You can cook it for a few minutes, then have a look and see how it's getting on – it won't spoil it.

4 Allow the pudding to stand for a few minutes, then turn out on to a warmed serving plate (or you could serve it straight from the bowl if you prefer), so that the golden syrupy top is uppermost, and decorate with the walnuts. Serve with extra maple syrup, if liked.

Once in a while it's nice to have a real indulgence and it's also fun to do some 'real' cooking in the microwave. I like to make this on a dreary winter's day, perhaps for Sunday lunch. It's so quick, you can do it on the spur of the moment.

No microwave?
If you don't have a microwave, you can steam the sponge mixture, but leaving out the milk or water. Make a pleat in a piece of foil, place over the top and sides of the bowl and tie with string around the rim of the bowl – or, much easier, use a plastic bowl with a snap-on lid. Put the basin in a steamer fitted over a saucepan of boiling water and steam for 1½ hours, checking the level of the water from time to time and topping up with boiling water if necessary.

SLIM FOR LIFE

My goal for this chapter was that the food be luxurious and appealing, helping you to get slim and stay slim without feeling deprived.

I've included some comforting, everyday dishes such as *Chunky bean and vegetable soup*, *Butter bean and herb mash with pak choy* and *Vanilla-poached figs* that are easy to make and won't leave you hungry. There are also more indulgent dishes, like *Green risotto with spinach, peas, herbs and runner beans*, *Omelette cannelloni with spinach filling* and *Cappuccino meringues* for when you want to spoil yourself or entertain. Good luck!

Carrot and caraway soup

PREPARATION 15 MINUTES COOKING 40 MINUTES SERVES 4

1 TABLESPOON OLIVE OIL • 1 ONION, CHOPPED • 1 BAKING POTATO, PEELED AND CUT INTO 1cm (½ inch) CUBES • 500g (1lb) SCRAPED CARROTS, SLICED • 2–3 STRIPS OF LEMON RIND • 1 TEASPOON CARAWAY SEEDS • 1.2 litres (2 pints) WATER OR LIGHT VEGETABLE STOCK • SALT AND PEPPER • FROMAGE FRAIS, NATURAL YOGURT OR REDUCED-FAT CRÈME FRAÎCHE (OPTIONAL), COARSELY GROUND BLACK PEPPER AND CHOPPED FLAT LEAF PARSLEY, TO SERVE

1 Heat the olive oil in a large saucepan. Add the onion, cover and fry gently for 5 minutes, stirring occasionally – don't let it brown.

2 Add the potato, cover and cook for a further 5 minutes, then add the carrots, lemon rind and caraway seeds. Stir well, then add the water or vegetable stock. Bring to the boil, cover and leave to cook gently for about 30 minutes, or until the carrots are very tender.

3 Purée the soup in a food processor or blender, then return it to the saucepan. Season with plenty of salt and a little pepper and reheat for serving.

4 Ladle the soup into bowls and swirl a teaspoon of fromage frais, yogurt or crème fraîche on top of each, if liked. Grind some pepper coarsely over the top, scatter with a little flat leaf parsley and serve.

Caraway, from the same plant family as carrots, gives this soup its subtle, unusual flavour and deserves to be more widely used. It also adds a lovely flavour to cooked, buttered carrots or beetroot.

Chunky bean and vegetable soup

PREPARATION 15 MINUTES COOKING 45 MINUTES SERVES 4

1 TABLESPOON OLIVE OIL • 2 ONIONS, CHOPPED • 250g (8oz) CARROTS, CUT INTO 1cm (½ inch) CHUNKS •

250g (8oz) PARSNIPS, CUT INTO 1cm (½ inch) CHUNKS • 250g (8oz) LEEKS, SLICED • 250g (8oz) CABBAGE, SLICED

• A FEW THYME SPRIGS • 2 BAY LEAVES • 410g (13½oz) CAN CANNELLINI BEANS, DRAINED • 1.2 litres (2 pints)

VEGETABLE STOCK • SALT AND PEPPER • CHOPPED PARSLEY, TO GARNISH • WHOLEMEAL BREAD AND GRATED

CHEESE, TO SERVE (OPTIONAL)

1 Heat the olive oil in a large saucepan, add the onions, cover and cook for 5 minutes. Then add the carrots, parsnips, leeks, cabbage, thyme and bay leaves and stir to lightly coat them all with the oil. Cover the pan and cook gently for a further 10 minutes.

2 Add the beans and vegetable stock, bring to the boil, then cover and leave to simmer over a gentle heat for 30 minutes. Season with salt and pepper, serve in warmed bowls and top each with a scattering of chopped parsley. Serve with wholemeal bread and grated cheese, if liked.

There are numerous versions of this Mediterranean soup which is easy to make and deliciously wholesome. Feel free to try using different vegetables or perhaps adding some small pasta shapes.

Spicy okra with red onions, mustard seeds and brown rice

PREPARATION 20 MINUTES COOKING 30 MINUTES SERVES 4

I TABLESPOON OLIVE OIL • 2 RED ONIONS, SLICED • 4 GARLIC CLOVES, CHOPPED • 4 TEASPOONS GROUND

CORIANDER • ½ TEASPOON TURMERIC • I TEASPOON MUSTARD SEEDS • 500g (IIb) OKRA, TRIMMED AND CUT

INTO 2.5cm (I inch) PIECES • 400g (13oz) CAN CHOPPED TOMATOES • ½ TEASPOON GARAM MASALA • SALT,

PEPPER AND SUGAR • CORIANDER LEAVES, TO GARNISH

RICE 250g (8oz) BROWN BASMATI RICE • 600ml (I pint) WATER

1 Put the rice and water into a heavy-based saucepan and bring to the boil. Cover the pan, then turn the heat down and cook over a very low heat for 20 minutes. Remove from the heat and leave to stand, still covered, until you're ready to serve.

2 To make the spicy okra, heat the olive oil in a large saucepan, add the onions, cover and fry for 10–15 minutes, until tender. Add the garlic, ground coriander, turmeric and mustard seeds and stir over the heat for a few seconds, until they smell aromatic.

3 Add the okra and stir to coat with the onion and spice mixture, then add the tomatoes. Cover and leave to cook gently for 15–20 minutes, or until the okra is very tender.

4 Stir in the garam masala, taste and season with salt, pepper and a dash of sugar if it needs it. Sprinkle with fresh coriander and serve with the rice.

Butter bean and herb mash with pak choi

PREPARATION 15 MINUTES COOKING 10 MINUTES SERVES 4

2 X 410g (13½oz) CANS BUTTER BEANS • 2 GARLIC CLOVES • 1–2 TABLESPOONS FRESHLY SQUEEZED LEMON JUICE • 4 SPRING ONIONS, CHOPPED • 2 TABLESPOONS CHOPPED PARSLEY • SALT AND PEPPER

PAK CHOI 500g (1lb) PAK CHOI OR OTHER ASIAN LEAVES, LARGE PIECES HALVED OR QUARTERED • 1 TABLESPOON SOY SAUCE • 1 TABLESPOON LEMON JUICE • 1 TABLESPOON TOASTED SESAME OIL • 1 TABLESPOON TOASTED SESAME SEEDS

1 Drain the butter beans, reserving the liquid. Either mash the beans roughly using a fork or potato masher or, for a smoother mash, whiz them in a food processor.

2 Put the mashed beans into a saucepan with the garlic, lemon juice, spring onions, parsley and enough of the reserved bean liquid to make the consistency of mashed potatoes. Season with salt and pepper. Heat gently and keep warm.

3 Put the pak choi or other leaves in 2.5cm (1 inch) depth of boiling water in a large saucepan. Cover and cook for 2–6 minutes, or until it's just tender – the timing will depend on the exact type of leaves and the size of the pieces. Drain in a colander, then return to the pan.

4 Add the soy sauce, lemon juice, sesame oil and sesame seeds to the leaves and swirl around to coat them all. Serve with the butter bean mash.

Lentils with portobellos, garlic and red wine

PREPARATION 15 MINUTES COOKING 30 MINUTES SERVES 4

1 TABLESPOON OLIVE OIL • 2 ONIONS, CHOPPED • 4 GARLIC CLOVES, FINELY CHOPPED • 8 PORTOBELLO
MUSHROOMS • 2 TOMATOES, CHOPPED • A FEW THYME SPRIGS • 2 BAY LEAVES • 410g (13½oz) CAN GREEN
LENTILS • 250ml (8fl oz) RED WINE • 2 TEASPOONS DIJON MUSTARD • SALT AND PEPPER • CHOPPED
PARSLEY, TO GARNISH

1 Heat the olive oil in a large saucepan, add the onions, cover and cook for 5 minutes. Add the garlic, mushrooms, tomatoes and herbs and stir until lightly coated with the oil. Cover the pan and cook gently for a further 10 minutes.

2 Add the lentils, together with their liquid, and the wine, bring to the boil, then cover and leave to simmer over a gentle heat for 30 minutes.

3 Put the mustard into a small bowl, add a little liquid from the pan and stir to make a smooth cream, then tip this into the pan and stir again. Season with salt and pepper. Garnish with the parsley and serve.

This is delicious with mashed potatoes or, for a lower-calorie version, try cauliflower mash (see page 99), or just lots of lightly cooked cabbage. If you prefer, you can use cooked Puy lentils instead of green lentils.

Green risotto with spinach, peas, herbs and runner beans

PREPARATION 30 MINUTES, PLUS STANDING COOKING 35 MINUTES SERVES 4

I TABLESPOON OLIVE OIL • I ONION, CHOPPED • I CELERY STICK, FINELY CHOPPED • 125g (4oz) RUNNER BEANS, TRIMMED AND CUT INTO 2.5cm (1 inch) LENGTHS • I TEASPOON VEGETABLE STOCK POWDER OR I CUBE • I LARGE GARLIC CLOVE, CRUSHED • 400g (13oz) RISOTTO RICE • 250ml (8fl oz) WHITE WINE • 125g (4oz) BABY LEAF SPINACH • 125g (4oz) FRESH OR FROZEN PETIT POIS • 3–4 TABLESPOONS CHOPPED HERBS – PARSLEY, MINT, DILL, CHIVES, WHATEVER IS AVAILABLE • SALT AND PEPPER • GRATED OR SHAVED PARMESAN CHEESE, TO SERVE (OPTIONAL)

1 Heat the olive oil in a large saucepan. Add the onion and celery, stir, then cover and cook for 7 minutes.

2 Meanwhile, cook the runner beans in boiling water to cover, for 4–5 minutes, or until just tender. Drain and set aside, reserving the liquid. Make the liquid up to 1.2 litres (2 pints) and put into a pan with the vegetable stock powder or cube. Bring to the boil and keep warm.

3 Add the garlic and rice to the onion and celery in the pan and stir well. Add half the white wine and continue cooking, stirring all the time, until the wine has bubbled away. Repeat the process with the remaining wine, then add the hot stock in the same way, a ladleful at a time.

4 When the rice is tender and all or most of the stock has been used up – about 25 minutes – add the spinach, reserved beans, peas and herbs, cover and leave to stand for 5 minutes, until the spinach is cooked.

5 Season with salt and pepper and serve at once with a little Parmesan, if you like.

It's hard to believe that such a delectable risotto is actually low in fat; roasted tomatoes complement it perfectly.

Tagliatelle of cabbage with cream cheese, herb and garlic sauce

PREPARATION 10 MINUTES COOKING 10 MINUTES SERVES 4

1kg (2lb) HEARTY PALE GREEN CABBAGE SUCH AS 'SWEETHEART' OR 'JANUARY KING', HARD CORE REMOVED AND LEAVES CUT INTO LONG STRANDS LIKE TAGLIATELLE • 250g (8oz) LOW-FAT SOFT CREAM CHEESE • 2 GARLIC CLOVES, CRUSHED • 4 TABLESPOONS CHOPPED PARSLEY AND CHIVES • GRATED RIND OF 1 LEMON • SALT AND PEPPER • SHAVED OR GRATED PARMESAN CHEESE, TO SERVE (OPTIONAL)

1 Half-fill a large saucepan with water and bring to the boil. Add the cabbage and cook, uncovered, for 5–6 minutes, or until tender. Drain and return the cabbage to the saucepan.

2 Add the cream cheese to the pan, along with the garlic, herbs, lemon rind and some salt and pepper to taste. Mix well gently, then serve on warmed plates topped with a little Parmesan, if you like.

Eggs in coconut curry sauce with cauliflower 'rice'

PREPARATION 20 MINUTES COOKING 15 MINUTES SERVES 4

1 TABLESPOON OLIVE OIL • 1 SMALL ONION, FINELY CHOPPED • 1 SMALL FRESH GREEN CHILLI, DESEEDED AND
SLICED • 2 GARLIC CLOVES, CRUSHED • 2 TEASPOONS GRATED FRESH ROOT GINGER • 2 TOMATOES, CHOPPED
• 2 TEASPOONS CORIANDER SEEDS • 4 CARDAMOM PODS • 400ml (14fl oz) CAN COCONUT MILK (SEE PAGE 41)
• 3 TABLESPOONS CHOPPED CORIANDER, PLUS EXTRA TO GARNISH • 8 HARD-BOILED EGGS, HALVED
CAULIFLOWER 'RICE' 1 CAULIFLOWER, TRIMMED AND CUT INTO FLORETS • SALT AND PEPPER

1 Heat the olive oil in a saucepan, add the onion, cover and cook for 5 minutes, then add the chilli, garlic, ginger and tomatoes. Stir and cook for a further 2–3 minutes.

2 Meanwhile, crush the coriander seeds and cardamom pods using a coffee grinder or pestle and mortar and add to the onion mixture. Stir for a few seconds, then add the coconut milk and cook over a gentle heat for a further 2–3 minutes. Stir in the coriander and season with salt and pepper.

3 Gently put the hard-boiled eggs into the coconut mixture, spooning it over them, and leave, covered, over a very gentle heat for the flavours to infuse while you deal with the cauliflower.

4 Bring 5cm (2 inches) depth of water to the boil in a large saucepan. Add the cauliflower, bring back to the boil, cover and cook for 4 minutes, until the cauliflower is just tender. Drain well.

5 Put the cauliflower into a food processor with some salt and pepper and whiz to a grainy texture – like cooked rice. Stop before it turns to mash! Return it to the saucepan and gently reheat, stirring so that it doesn't catch. Garnish the egg curry with the remaining coriander and serve with the cauliflower 'rice'.

Omelette cannelloni with spinach filling

PREPARATION 20 MINUTES COOKING 40 MINUTES SERVES 4

750g (1½ lb) SPINACH, WASHED • 125g (4oz) LOW-FAT SOFT CREAM CHEESE • 8 TABLESPOONS FRESHLY GRATED

PARMESAN CHEESE • GRATED NUTMEG • 4 EGGS • 2 TABLESPOONS WATER • 1 TABLESPOON OLIVE OIL •

SALT AND PEPPER

1 Put the spinach with just the water clinging to the leaves into a large saucepan, cover and cook for 6–7 minutes, or until tender. Drain well.

2 Add the cream cheese to the spinach along with 4 tablespoons of the Parmesan. Mix well and season with salt, pepper and grated nutmeg. Set aside.

3 Whisk the eggs with the water and salt and pepper to taste. Brush a frying pan (preferably nonstick) with a little of the olive oil and heat, then pour in enough of the egg – about 2 tablespoons – to make a small omelette. Cook for a few seconds, until it is set, then lift out on to a plate. Continue in this way until you have made about 8 small omelettes, piling them up on top of each other.

4 Spoon a little of the spinach mixture on to the edge of one of the omelettes, roll it up and place in a shallow gratin dish. Fill the remaining omelettes in the same way, until all the spinach mixture is used, placing them snugly side by side in the dish. Sprinkle with the remaining Parmesan and bake in a preheated oven, 190°C (375°F), Gas Mark 5, for about 25 minutes, or until bubbling and golden brown on top.

This is delicious – an excellent dish if you're trying to lose weight, whether you're counting calories or carbs.

Chunky lentil, onion and chestnut loaf with sherry gravy

PREPARATION 20 MINUTES COOKING I HOUR 20 MINUTES SERVES 4

125g (4oz) SPLIT RED LENTILS • 300ml (½ pint) WATER • I BAY LEAF • I TEASPOON OLIVE OIL • I ONION, CHOPPED • 3 GARLIC CLOVES, CHOPPED • I CELERY STICK, CHOPPED • 2 TOMATOES, CHOPPED • 240g (8oz) VACUUM-PACKED CHESTNUTS • I TEASPOON SOY SAUCE • SALT AND PEPPER
GRAVY 600ml (I pint) WATER • I TABLESPOON VEGETARIAN STOCK POWDER • 3 TABLESPOONS SOY SAUCE • 1½ TABLESPOONS REDCURRANT JELLY • I TABLESPOON CORNFLOUR • 1½ TABLESPOONS ORANGE JUICE • 1½ TABLESPOONS SHERRY • SALT AND PEPPER

1 Line a 500g (1lb) loaf tin with a strip of nonstick baking paper to cover the base and extend up the narrow sides.

2 Put the red lentils in a saucepan with the water and bay leaf. Bring to the boil, then turn down the heat and leave to simmer gently for 15–20 minutes, or until the lentils are tender and all the water has been absorbed.

3 Meanwhile, heat the olive oil in a pan, add the onion and fry for 10 minutes, stirring often to prevent sticking. Remove from the heat and add to the lentils, along with the garlic, celery, tomatoes, chestnuts, soy sauce and some salt and pepper.

4 Spoon the lentil mixture into the loaf tin, press down well and smooth the surface. Bake in a preheated oven, 200°C (400°F), Gas Mark 6, for 1 hour, until firm.

5 Meanwhile, make the gravy. Put the water, stock powder, soy sauce and redcurrant jelly into a saucepan and bring to the boil. Blend the cornflour with the orange juice and sherry. Stir a little of the hot liquid into the cornflour mixture, then tip this into the saucepan. Stir well, then simmer over a gentle heat until slightly thickened and season to taste with salt and pepper.

6 Loosen the edges of the lentil loaf by slipping a knife down the sides, then invert the tin over a plate and turn the loaf out. Serve in thick slices, with the gravy.

Thai-flavoured slaw

PREPARATION 10 MINUTES COOKING 2–3 MINUTES SERVES 4

½ SMALL CABBAGE, ABOUT 275g (9oz) • SMALL BUNCH OF CORIANDER, ROUGHLY CHOPPED • 4 SPRING ONIONS, CHOPPED • I MILD RED CHILLI, DESEEDED AND CHOPPED • 2 TABLESPOONS RICE VINEGAR • I TABLESPOON MIRIN OR I TEASPOON CLEAR HONEY • I TABLESPOON SESAME SEEDS • SALT

1 Cut the cabbage half into two halves, cut away and discard the hard inner core, then shred the cabbage finely with a sharp knife and put into a bowl.

2 To make the light dressing, add the coriander, spring onions and chilli to the bowl, then stir in the rice vinegar, mirin or honey and season with salt.

3 Toast the sesame seeds by putting them into a small dry saucepan and stirring over a moderate heat for a minute or two until they begin to turn golden brown and smell delicious, then scatter over the top of the salad.

This salad can be made in advance if you like; the cabbage will soften in the tasty, oil-free dressing.

Quinoa and red grape salad with honey dressing and toasted almonds

PREPARATION 15 MINUTES COOKING 20 MINUTES SERVES 4

175g (6oz) QUINOA • 450ml (¾ pint) WATER • 2 TABLESPOONS FLAKED ALMONDS • 250g (8oz) SEEDLESS RED GRAPES, HALVED • 3–4 SPRING ONIONS, CHOPPED • 4 TEASPOONS CLEAR HONEY • 4 TEASPOONS CIDER VINEGAR • SALT AND PEPPER • LITTLE GEM LETTUCE LEAVES AND WATERCRESS, TO SERVE

1 Put the quinoa into a saucepan with the water. Bring to the boil, then cover and cook gently for 15 minutes, until the quinoa is tender. Remove from the heat and leave to stand, covered, for a few more minutes, or until cold.

2 Spread the flaked almonds out on a grill pan or shallow roasting tin that will fit under the grill. Put under a preheated hot grill for a minute or so until they turn golden. Give them a stir if necessary so they cook evenly, but watch them like a hawk as they burn very easily. As soon as they're done, remove them from the grill and transfer to a plate, to ensure they don't go on cooking in the residual heat.

3 Put the quinoa into a bowl with the grapes, spring onions, honey, cider vinegar and some salt and pepper and mix gently. This can be done in advance if you like.

4 Just before serving, stir in the flaked almonds. It's especially nice if they're still slightly warm from the grill. Serve with some crunchy little gem lettuce leaves, perhaps mixed with some watercress.

Mediterranean stuffed peppers with cauliflower mash

PREPARATION 10 MINUTES COOKING 30 MINUTES SERVES 4

4 RED PEPPERS, SUCH AS RAMIRO • 200g (7oz) FETA CHEESE, CUT INTO 1cm (½ inch) CUBES • 8 HEAPED

TEASPOONS PESTO • 16 CHERRY TOMATOES, HALVED

CAULIFLOWER MASH 1 CAULIFLOWER, TRIMMED AND CUT INTO FLORETS • 25g (1oz) BUTTER • SALT AND PEPPER

1 Halve the peppers, cutting right through the stems too if you can. Trim the insides and rinse away all the seeds. Put the peppers in a roasting tin or large shallow casserole dish. Divide the feta between the peppers, then spoon over the pesto. Finally top with the tomatoes, skin-side up.

2 Bake in a preheated oven, 200°C (400°F), Gas Mark 6, for 30 minutes, or until the tops are charring and the insides full of luscious juice.

3 Meanwhile, make the cauliflower mash. Bring 5cm (2 inches) depth of water to the boil in a large saucepan. Add the cauliflower, bring back to the boil, cover and cook for 5–6 minutes, until the cauliflower is tender. Drain well. Put the cauliflower into a food processor with the butter and some salt and pepper and whiz to a smooth, thick mixture. Return to the saucepan and gently reheat, stirring so that it doesn't catch, then serve with the peppers.

The cauliflower mash is like a very light version of mashed potatoes but with a fraction of the calories. It's also low in carbs and a good way of getting one of the daily 'five portions' of fruit and vegetables – cauliflower counts as a portion but potatoes don't. You could also serve these peppers with cauliflower 'rice' (see page 93).

Cappuccino meringues

PREPARATION 15 MINUTES COOKING 2 HOURS MAKES 12 HALVES

2 EGG WHITES • 1 TEASPOON GOOD-QUALITY INSTANT COFFEE GRANULES • 125g (4oz) CASTER SUGAR

FILLING 150ml (¼ pint) FROMAGE FRAIS, LOW-FAT CRÈME FRAÎCHE OR THICK GREEK YOGURT • DRINKING

CHOCOLATE POWDER, TO DECORATE

1 Line a baking sheet with a strip of nonstick baking paper.

2 Put the egg whites and instant coffee granules into a clean, grease-free mixing bowl and whisk until very thick – the peaks formed must be able to hold their shape and you should be able to turn the bowl upside down without the mixture coming out. However, don't get it to the point where the whisked eggs start to break up and lose their volume. Add the caster sugar a tablespoon at a time, whisking after each addition.

3 Put heaped dessertspoonfuls of the mixture on to the baking paper, leaving a little space between them, then put into a preheated oven, 120°C (250°F), Gas Mark ½, and cook for 2 hours, until they have dried out. If possible, switch off the heat and leave them in the oven to get completely cold.

4 Just before serving the meringues, sandwich pairs together with a good spoonful of your chosen filling, put on a plate and sprinkle with a little chocolate powder. Eat within about 2 hours.

Meringues are a wonderful fat-free treat and easy to make; the filling can be as indulgent or virtuous as you like.

Vanilla-poached figs

PREPARATION 10 MINUTES COOKING 30 MINUTES SERVES 4

450ml (¾ pint) WATER • 3 TABLESPOONS CASTER SUGAR • 2 VANILLA PODS • 8 FRESH FIGS • 250g (8oz) THICK NATURAL YOGURT, TO SERVE (OPTIONAL)

1 Make a light syrup: put the water, caster sugar and vanilla pods into a saucepan large enough to take the figs, bring to the boil and simmer for 5 minutes.

2 Add the figs to the pan. Bring to the boil, then cover and cook over a gentle heat for 20 minutes, or until the figs are plump and very tender when pierced with the point of a sharp knife.

3 Remove the figs from the pan with a slotted spoon. In each fig, make a cut lengthways, almost to the bottom of the fruit, then another cut perpendicular to it. Place in a shallow serving dish. Boil the syrup and vanilla pods hard for a few minutes until it has reduced a little and thickened. Pour the syrup over the figs. Serve hot, warm or cold, with natural yogurt, if liked.

A wonderful way to turn less-than-perfect figs into a plump, succulent treat. The vanilla pods can be used again. Remove them after use, rinse under the tap and leave to dry. A good way to store them is buried in a jar of caster sugar, this absorbs their flavour and keeps them dry.

WORLD FOOD

In my quest for new recipes, I find great inspiration from the food of other countries. I particularly love the dishes of India and the Middle East – these countries, with their wonderfully inventive use of lentils, beans, grains, vegetables, herbs and spices, are fabulous places for vegetarians and vegans to visit. I also love Thai and Indonesian food, and that of Japan, with its piquant dips and marinades, fresh crisp vegetables and copious use of tofu, which I adore.

In this chapter I've used ideas, recipes and ingredients from all of these places, and others. I do hope you'll enjoy trying them.

Coulibiac with soured cream sauce

PREPARATION 20 MINUTES COOKING 55 MINUTES SERVES 4

125g (4oz) BASMATI RICE • I TABLESPOON OLIVE OIL • 25g (1oz) BUTTER • I LARGE ONION, FINELY CHOPPED • 175g (6oz) GREEN CABBAGE, SHREDDED • 250g (8oz) BABY BUTTON MUSHROOMS, HALVED • 3 HARD-BOILED EGGS, ROUGHLY CHOPPED • 4 TABLESPOONS CHOPPED DILL • 2 X 350g (12oz) SHEETS OF READY-ROLLED PUFF PASTRY • I EGG, BEATEN, FOR GLAZING • MALDON SEA SALT FLAKES • SALT AND PEPPER
SAUCE 4 TABLESPOONS CHOPPED CHIVES • 300ml (½ pint) SOURED CREAM

1 Cook the rice in plenty of fast-boiling water for about 10 minutes, or until tender, then drain and set aside.

2 Meanwhile, heat the olive oil and butter in a large saucepan, add the onion, cover and cook for 5 minutes. Add the cabbage and mushrooms, stir, cover and cook for about 10 minutes, or until the cabbage is tender. Remove from the heat.

3 Add the drained rice, the eggs and dill to the onion mixture and season with salt and pepper. Allow to cool a little.

4 Put the two sheets of puff pastry side by side on a large baking sheet and press them lightly together where they meet, to make one large piece. Trim 4cm (1½ inches) off the sides of the pastry.

5 Spoon the rice mixture along the centre of the piece of pastry, on top of the join. Make diagonal cuts in the pastry on each side of the rice filling and fold them alternately over the filling to create a plaited effect; trim off any excess pastry. Brush with beaten egg and sprinkle with the sea salt. Bake in a preheated oven, 200°C (400°F), Gas Mark 6, for 40 minutes, or until the coulibiac is puffy and golden brown.

6 To make the sauce, stir the chives into the soured cream and season with salt and pepper. Serve with the coulibiac.

This makes a lovely spring or summer meal, served with baby new potatoes and buttered baby beans or courgettes. For a special occasion it's also nice served with hollandaise sauce (see page 21).

Vegetarian pad thai

PREPARATION 20 MINUTES COOKING 20 MINUTES SERVES 4

250g (8oz) RICE NOODLES • RAPESEED OIL FOR DEEP-FRYING • 2 X 250g (8oz) BLOCKS OF TOFU, EACH CUT INTO 1cm (½ inch) CUBES • 2 TABLESPOONS ROASTED SESAME OIL • 2 ONIONS, CHOPPED • 4 GARLIC CLOVES, FINELY CHOPPED • 4 TEASPOONS TAMARIND PURÉE • 2 TABLESPOONS SOY SAUCE • 2 TEASPOONS BROWN SUGAR • 125g (4oz) BEAN SPROUTS • 2 EGGS, BEATEN • 25–50g (1–2oz) ROASTED PEANUTS, LIGHTLY CRUSHED • SALT AND PEPPER • ROUGHLY CHOPPED CORIANDER, TO GARNISH

1 Put the noodles in a bowl, cover with boiling water and leave to soak until tender – the timing depends on the thickness of the noodles; very fine ones take 5 minutes, thicker ones take longer. Drain.

2 Heat the rapeseed oil in a wok to 180–190°C (350–375°F) or until a cube of bread browns in 30 seconds. Add the tofu and deep-fry for about 5 minutes. Remove and set aside.

3 Heat all but 1 teaspoon of the sesame oil in a large saucepan. Add the onions and fry for 7–10 minutes, until tender, then stir in the garlic. Cook for a few seconds, then stir in the deep-fried tofu, tamarind purée, soy sauce, brown sugar, bean sprouts and drained noodles. Cook over the heat for 2–3 minutes until the bean sprouts are tender and everything is heated through.

4 While this is happening, heat the remaining sesame oil in a frying pan, pour in the eggs and make an omelette, pulling back the edges of the omelette as it sets and tipping the pan so that uncooked egg runs to the edges. When the omelette is set, roll it up, put it on a plate, cut into shreds and add to the noodles.

5 Season the noodle mixture to taste with salt and pepper, then serve on warmed plates and top with the crushed peanuts and a generous amount of coriander.

You can buy deep-fried tofu, or make your own by cutting the tofu into cubes and deep-frying in a little rapeseed or groundnut oil for 6–7 minutes, until golden brown.

Agedashi tofu

PREPARATION 15 MINUTES COOKING 20 MINUTES SERVES 4

RAPESEED OIL FOR DEEP-FRYING • 2 X 250g (8oz) BLOCKS OF FRESH TOFU, EACH DRAINED AND CUT INTO

1cm (½ inch) CUBES • 1–2 TABLESPOONS CORNFLOUR, ARROWROOT OR KUZU • 1–2 SPRING ONIONS, CUT

INTO SHREDS, TO GARNISH

BROTH 1 litre (1¾ pints) WATER • PIECE OF KOMBU SEAWEED • 1 TEASPOON VEGETARIAN BOUILLON POWDER

• 1–3 TEASPOONS UNPASTEURIZED BARLEY-SOY MISO • 4 SPRING ONIONS, FINELY CHOPPED

1 First make the broth. Heat the water and kombu in a large saucepan. When it comes to the boil, remove the kombu – this can be dried and used again. Add the bouillon powder and set aside.

2 For the tofu, heat the rapeseed oil in a wok to 180°C (350°F). While it's heating, put the tofu on to a plate, sprinkle with the cornflour, arrowroot or kuzu (crushed to remove lumps) and toss, so that the powder sticks to the damp surfaces of the tofu. Lower the tofu into the oil – you may need to do more than one batch so that you don't overcrowd the pan. Fry for about 6 minutes, until the tofu is crisp and golden, then drain on kitchen paper.

3 Reheat the broth and when it comes to the boil take it off the heat and stir in the miso, to taste. (If it boils again after this, some of the health-giving properties of the miso are destroyed.)

4 Serve the tofu on to 4 warmed plates and garnish with the shredded spring onions. Divide the chopped spring onions between 4 bowls, ladle the broth on top and serve accompanied by the tofu.

This dish, which I love, consists of crisp, deep-fried tofu with a bowl of miso broth. To experience this at its best, you do need to use real Asian (preferably Japanese) tofu, which is delicate and almost 'wobbly' in consistency – in fact, I prefer this kind of tofu for all recipes.

Sweet potato and coconut dal with coriander

PREPARATION 15 MINUTES COOKING 20 MINUTES SERVES 4

550g (1lb 2oz) ORANGE-FLESHED SWEET POTATO, PEELED AND CUT INTO 1cm (½ inch) CUBES • 175g (6oz) SPLIT RED LENTILS • 1 GREEN CHILLI, DESEEDED AND SLICED • 400ml (14fl oz) CAN COCONUT MILK (SEE PAGE 41) • 450ml (¾ pint) WATER • 1 TEASPOON GRATED FRESH ROOT GINGER • 1 TEASPOON GROUND CINNAMON • ½ TEASPOON TURMERIC • SALT AND PEPPER • CHOPPED CORIANDER, TO GARNISH

1 Put the sweet potato into a saucepan with the lentils, chilli, coconut milk and water. Bring to the boil, then leave to cook gently, uncovered, for 15–20 minutes, until the sweet potato and lentils are tender and the mixture looks thick.

2 Stir in the ginger, cinnamon, turmeric and some salt and pepper to taste, then cook gently for a few more minutes to blend in the flavours. Sprinkle with coriander and serve with some lightly cooked cabbage, plain-cooked rice or cauliflower 'rice' (see page 93).

This is delicious – and tastes even better the next day. Note that the spices are added after the lentils are tender – if you add them at the beginning, they can prevent the lentils from becoming tender, as can tomatoes or anything acidic.

Creamy cashew korma

PREPARATION 20 MINUTES COOKING 40 MINUTES SERVES 4

I TABLESPOON RAPESEED OIL • I LARGE ONION, FINELY CHOPPED • 2 GARLIC CLOVES, CRUSHED • I TEASPOON TURMERIC • I TABLESPOON GROUND CUMIN • I TABLESPOON GROUND CORIANDER • 50g (2oz) CASHEW NUTS • 400ml (14fl oz) CAN COCONUT MILK (SEE PAGE 41) • 400ml (14fl oz) WATER • SMALL HANDFUL OF FRESH CURRY LEAVES (OPTIONAL) • 175g (6oz) OKRA, TOPPED AND TAILED • 250g (8oz) CAULIFLOWER FLORETS • 250g (8oz) BROCCOLI FLORETS • SALT AND PEPPER • CHOPPED CORIANDER LEAVES, TO GARNISH

1 Heat the rapeseed oil in a large saucepan. Add the onion, cover and fry for about 10 minutes, or until tender. Stir in the garlic, turmeric, cumin and ground coriander, and cook for a minute or two longer.

2 Grind the cashew nuts to a powder in a coffee grinder, food processor or using the fine grater in a hand mill. Add them to the pan, along with the coconut milk.

3 For a really smooth sauce, you can now purée the whole lot in a food processor or blender (or use a stick blender in the saucepan) or, if you prefer some texture, leave it as it is.

4 Return the mixture to the pan, if you've puréed it, and add the water and curry leaves, if using. Leave to simmer for 20–30 minutes, stirring from time to time, until thickened.

5 Just before the sauce is ready, put the okra, cauliflower and broccoli into a pan containing a depth of 5cm (2 inches) boiling water. Cover and cook for about 6 minutes, or until tender. Drain, and add the vegetables to the korma, stirring gently. Season with salt and pepper.

6 You can serve this at once, but if there's time, let it rest for a while – even overnight – for the flavours to intensify. Then gently reheat. Scatter with coriander before serving and serve with hot white basmati rice.

An electric coffee grinder is quite inexpensive and is invaluable for turning nuts into powder in an instant, and also for grinding spices – it's one of my favourite pieces of equipment.

Refried beans

PREPARATION 15 MINUTES COOKING 15 MINUTES SERVES 4

2 TABLESPOONS OLIVE OIL • 1 LARGE ONION, FINELY CHOPPED • 2 GARLIC CLOVES, CHOPPED • 2 X 410g (13½oz) CANS PINTO BEANS, DRAINED • ½–1 TEASPOON CHILLI POWDER • SALT AND PEPPER TO SERVE LETTUCE LEAVES • SLICED TOMATOES • 1 LARGE AVOCADO, PEELED, STONED AND SLICED • SOURED CREAM • PAPRIKA • CHOPPED CORIANDER • TORTILLA CHIPS • GRATED CHEDDAR CHEESE (OPTIONAL)

1 Heat the olive oil in a large, heavy-based saucepan, add the onion, cover and cook gently for 10 minutes, stirring from time to time. Stir in the garlic and cook for a minute or two longer.

2 Add the pinto beans to the pan, along with the chilli powder, salt and pepper to taste. Mash the beans roughly with a potato masher or wooden spoon so that they cling together, but keep plenty of texture. Stir well so that they don't stick to the pan. The beans are ready when they're piping hot.

3 Arrange some lettuce leaves on a large serving plate and spoon the beans into the centre. Arrange tomato and avocado slices around the edge, swirl soured cream, paprika and coriander on top and serve with tortilla chips and grated Cheddar, if liked.

It's all the extras that make this very simple dish special. I like to serve them in little bowls so everyone can help themselves to what they want.

South American pinto and pumpkin casserole

PREPARATION 15 MINUTES COOKING 15 MINUTES SERVES 4

500g (1lb) SKINNED AND DESEEDED PUMPKIN, CUT INTO 1cm (½ inch) CUBES • 4 GARLIC CLOVES •
900ml (1½ pints) VEGETABLE STOCK • 1 TABLESPOON OLIVE OIL • 2 LARGE ONIONS, FINELY CHOPPED •
2 LARGE RED PEPPERS, CORED, DESEEDED AND DICED • 2 TEASPOONS DRIED EPAZOTE OR BASIL • KERNELS
CUT FROM 1 SWEETCORN COB, OR 150g (5oz) FROZEN SWEETCORN • 2 X 410g (13½oz) CANS PINTO BEANS •
2–3 TABLESPOONS LEMON JUICE • SALT AND PEPPER • 1 TABLESPOON FINELY CHOPPED FRESH EPAZOTE OR
FLAT LEAF PARSLEY, TO GARNISH

1 Put the cubes of pumpkin into a large saucepan with the garlic and vegetable stock. Bring to the boil, cover and simmer for about 15 minutes, or until the pumpkin is very tender. Then tip the contents of the pan into a food processor and whiz to a thin purée.

2 While the pumpkin is cooking, heat the olive oil in another large saucepan. Add the onions, peppers and dried epazote or basil. Cover the pan and fry over a gentle heat for 15 minutes, or until the vegetables are tender and slightly caramelized.

3 Add the pumpkin purée to the vegetables in the pan, along with the sweetcorn kernels and the pinto beans and their liquid. Stir over a gentle heat until hot, then add the lemon juice and salt and pepper to taste.

4 Ladle into warmed bowls, sprinkle with fresh epazote or parsley and serve with warm country bread (I love a dark wholemeal or walnut bread with this – not very South American, but very good!).

Vietnamese spring rolls

PREPARATION 30 MINUTES SERVES 4

50g (2oz) THIN RICE NOODLES (ONE BUNDLE FROM A PACKET) • 150g (5oz) BEAN SPROUTS • 1 RED PEPPER, CORED, DESEEDED AND FINELY SLICED • 2 TEASPOONS CHOPPED MINT • 2 TEASPOONS CHOPPED CORIANDER • 3 SPRING ONIONS, FINELY CHOPPED • 3 TABLESPOONS TERIYAKI SAUCE • 8 RICE FLOUR PANCAKES

PEANUT DIP 2 TABLESPOONS CRUNCHY PEANUT BUTTER • 2 TEASPOONS BROWN SUGAR • 1cm (½ inch) PIECE OF FRESH ROOT GINGER, GRATED • 1 GARLIC CLOVE, CRUSHED • ⅛–¼ TEASPOON DRIED RED CHILLI FLAKES • 6–8 TABLESPOONS SOY SAUCE

1 Put the rice noodles into a bowl, cover with boiling water and leave to soak for 5 minutes to soften, then drain well and place in a bowl.

2 Add the bean sprouts, red pepper, mint, coriander, spring onions and teriyaki sauce and mix well, making sure the ingredients are well distributed.

3 Spread a clean damp tea towel over your work surface. Put the rice pancakes into a bowl, cover with hot water and leave to soak for about 20 seconds, or until they become flexible. Remove them from the water and spread them out on the tea towel.

4 Take about 2 tablespoons of the bean sprout mixture and place on one of the pancakes towards the edge nearest you. Fold in the two sides, then the bottom edge so that it covers the filling. Roll this over again, holding in the filling firmly, and keep rolling until you have a firmly packed spring roll. Put this on a plate, seam-side down. Continue in this way until all the pancakes have been used. Cover the finished rolls with the clean damp tea towel until required.

5 To make the dip, mix together the peanut butter, sugar, ginger, garlic and chilli, then gradually mix in the soy sauce. Put into 4 small bowls and serve with the spring rolls.

These unusual spring rolls are made from rice pancakes and are served uncooked, with a spicy dipping sauce. They taste very fresh and delicious; serve as a starter or snack, or with Sesame-roasted tofu (see page 60) and rice.

Indonesian savoury stuffed pineapples

PREPARATION 20 MINUTES COOKING 45 MINUTES SERVES 4

300g (10oz) BASMATI RICE • 600ml (1 pint) WATER • 2 SMALL PINEAPPLES WITH LEAFY TOPS • 1 TABLESPOON SESAME OIL • 1 ONION, CHOPPED • 100g (3½oz) WHOLE CASHEW NUTS, TOASTED UNDER THE GRILL • 125g (4oz) FROZEN PETIT POIS, THAWED • 2–4 TABLESPOONS KETJAP MANIS (SEE BELOW) • 2 TEASPOONS BROWN SUGAR • 3 TABLESPOONS DESICCATED COCONUT, TOASTED UNDER THE GRILL

1 Put the rice into a saucepan with the water. Bring to the boil, then cover, reduce the heat and leave to cook gently for 15 minutes, until the rice is tender and all the water has been absorbed.

2 Halve the pineapples lengthways, cutting right down through the leaves. Cut around the inside edge of the pineapple about 5mm (¼ inch) away from the skin and scoop out the flesh. Discard the hard core. Chop the flesh into 5mm (¼ inch) pieces.

3 Heat the sesame oil in a saucepan, add the onion, cover and cook gently for 10 minutes, until tender. Remove from the heat and stir in 4 heaped tablespoons of the cooked rice together with the pineapple flesh, cashews, petit pois, ketjap manis and the sugar. Taste and add a little more ketjap manis if necessary.

4 Pile the cashew mixture into the pineapple shells, heaping them up well and sprinkle the tops with the desiccated coconut. Put the stuffed pineapples into a shallow casserole dish or roasting tin and cover with tin foil. Bake in a preheated oven, 180°C (350°F), Gas Mark 4 for 30 minutes. After 20 minutes, put the remaining rice in a casserole dish, cover and place in the oven to reheat. Serve immediately.

Ketjap manis is an Indonesian soy sauce, which is sweeter and less salty than other types. If you can't get it, just use normal soy sauce and a teaspoon of brown sugar or a dash of honey.

Pakora vegetables with mint raita and lime

PREPARATION 15 MINUTES COOKING 15 MINUTES SERVES 4

250g (8oz) BROCCOLI, THINLY SLICED • 1 COURGETTE, THINLY SLICED • 1 RED ONION, THINLY SLICED •

1 SMALL RED PEPPER, CORED, DESEEDED AND THINLY SLICED • LIME WEDGES, TO SERVE

BATTER 250g (8oz) GRAM FLOUR • 1 TEASPOON SALT • 2 TEASPOONS BAKING POWDER • 2 TEASPOONS

CUMIN SEEDS • 300ml (½ pint) SPARKLING WATER • RAPESEED OIL FOR DEEP-FRYING

MINT RAITA 300g (10oz) NATURAL YOGURT (DAIRY OR VEGAN) • 4 TABLESPOONS CHOPPED MINT •

SALT AND PEPPER

1 To make the batter, sift the gram flour, salt and baking powder into a bowl. Add the cumin seeds, then pour in the fizzy water, stirring all the time, to make a batter the consistency of pouring cream. You can leave the batter to stand for an hour or so if you wish.

2 Make the raita by mixing the yogurt with the mint and seasoning with salt and pepper to taste. Put into a serving bowl and set aside.

3 Heat the rapeseed oil for deep-frying to 180–190°C (350–375°F) or until a cube of bread browns in 30 seconds.

4 Dip pieces of vegetable into the batter to coat, then drop them into the oil, adding only enough pieces to cover the surface of the oil. When they're golden brown – in about 4 minutes – remove them with a slotted spoon and drain on kitchen paper. Continue until all the vegetables have been cooked.

5 Garnish the pakora vegetables with lime wedges and serve immediately, with the bowl of raita.

Tandoori paneer

PREPARATION 10 MINUTES COOKING 10–15 MINUTES SERVES 4

2 X 225g (7½oz) BLOCKS OF PANEER, EACH CUT INTO 1cm (½ inch) CUBES • 2 TABLESPOONS ROUGHLY CHOPPED CORIANDER • SALT

SPICE MIXTURE 1 TABLESPOON GRATED FRESH ROOT GINGER (OR USE THE LAZY STUFF FROM A JAR) • 1 TABLESPOON CRUSHED GARLIC (OR USE THE LAZY STUFF FROM A JAR) • ½ TEASPOON HOT PAPRIKA OR CHILLI POWDER • 1 TEASPOON TURMERIC • 1 TABLESPOON GROUND CUMIN • 2 TABLESPOONS RAPESEED OIL • 2 TABLESPOONS LEMON JUICE

VEGETABLE GARNISH 4 TOMATOES, SLICED • 1 SMALL ONION, SLICED • 1 GREEN PEPPER, CORED, DESEEDED AND SLICED • LEMON WEDGES, WARM NAAN BREAD AND MINT RAITA (SEE PAGE 125), TO SERVE

1 To make the spice mixture, put all the ingredients into a bowl and mix together.

2 Toss the cubes of paneer in the spice mixture and stir to coat them, adding a little salt to taste, remembering that paneer is quite salty.

3 Spread the cubes of paneer out on a grill pan or on a baking sheet that will fit under your grill and cook under a preheated grill for 10–15 minutes, turning them a couple of times, until sizzling and crisp.

4 Meanwhile, to make the garnish, mix together the tomatoes, onion and green pepper and put into a serving bowl or on to individual plates. Serve the paneer straight from the grill, hot and sizzling, with the salad garnish, a scattering of coriander on top and lemon wedges. Eat with warm naan bread and some mint raita.

You need a lot of ingredients for this really quick and simple recipe and it's always popular! You can also make a very good vegan version by using firm tofu instead of paneer (see page 189).

Corn fritters with tomato sauce

PREPARATION 15 MINUTES COOKING 15 MINUTES SERVES 4

250g (8oz) SWEETCORN KERNELS, FRESHLY CUT FROM THE COB, FROZEN, OR DRAINED UNSWEETENED CANNED

• 1 EGG, SEPARATED • 25g (1oz) FINE WHOLEMEAL FLOUR • RAPESEED OIL FOR SHALLOW-FRYING

TOMATO SAUCE 1 TABLESPOON OLIVE OIL • 1 ONION, FINELY CHOPPED • 2 GARLIC CLOVES, CHOPPED •

400g (13oz) CAN CHOPPED TOMATOES • SALT AND PEPPER

1 First make the tomato sauce. Heat the olive oil in a saucepan and fry the onion for 7–10 minutes until tender. Stir in the garlic, then add the tomatoes and simmer for about 15 minutes or until all the extra liquid has gone. For a smoother texture, purée in a food processor or blender. Season with salt and pepper and set aside.

2 To make the fritters, put the sweetcorn into a bowl with the egg yolk, wholemeal flour and some salt and pepper and mix well. Whisk the egg white until it stands in stiff peaks, then gently fold into the sweetcorn mixture.

3 Heat a little rapeseed oil in a frying pan, then drop tablespoons of the sweetcorn mixture into the oil and fry on both sides until crisp. Drain the fritters on kitchen paper. Keep the first batch warm under a preheated grill or in a cool oven while you make the rest, then serve with the tomato sauce.

Chickpea tagine with fruity couscous

PREPARATION 15 MINUTES COOKING 30 MINUTES SERVES 4

2 TABLESPOONS OLIVE OIL • 2 ONIONS, CHOPPED • 2 GARLIC CLOVES, CRUSHED • 1 TEASPOON GROUND GINGER • 1 TEASPOON TURMERIC • ½ TEASPOON SAFFRON THREADS • 2 FENNEL BULBS, QUARTERED • 1 COURGETTE, ABOUT 250g (8oz), CUT INTO BATONS • 1 AUBERGINE, ABOUT 250g (8oz), CUT INTO 1cm (½ inch) DICE • 400g (13oz) CAN TOMATOES • 410g (13½oz) CAN CHICKPEAS, DRAINED • 125–250g (4–8oz) GREEN OLIVES, PITTED • 1 PRESERVED LEMON, RINSED IN COLD WATER AND CHOPPED, OR 1 THIN-SKINNED LEMON, FINELY SLICED • 300ml (½ pint) VEGETABLE STOCK • SALT AND PEPPER • 1 HEAPED TABLESPOON ROUGHLY CHOPPED CORIANDER, TO GARNISH

FRUITY COUSCOUS 375g (12oz) COUSCOUS • 1 TABLESPOON OLIVE OIL • 450ml (¾ pint) WATER • 50g (2oz) SULTANAS • 50g (2oz) DRIED APRICOTS, CHOPPED

1 Heat the olive oil in a large, heavy-based saucepan, add the onions, cover and cook gently for 10 minutes, stirring from time to time. Stir in the garlic and cook for a minute or two longer.

2 Add the ginger, turmeric and saffron to the pan and stir, then put in the fennel, courgette and aubergine. Stir for a minute or two, then add the tomatoes, chickpeas, olives, lemon and vegetable stock. Bring to the boil, then cover and leave to simmer for about 15 minutes, or until the vegetables are tender. Season with salt and pepper.

3 While the tagine is cooking, put the couscous into a saucepan with the olive oil, water, sultanas and apricots and bring to the boil. Cover and simmer for 5 minutes, then remove from the heat and leave to stand, covered, until required. Fluff with a fork, serve with the tagine and garnish with coriander.

Falafel with lemon sauce

PREPARATION 15 MINUTES, PLUS SOAKING COOKING 15 MINUTES SERVES 4

275g (9oz) DRIED CHICKPEAS • 1 SMALL ONION, ROUGHLY CHOPPED • 15g (½oz) CORIANDER • 2 GARLIC CLOVES, ROUGHLY CHOPPED • 1 TABLESPOON GROUND CUMIN • ½ TEASPOON BICARBONATE OF SODA • 1½ TEASPOONS SALT • 2 TABLESPOONS GRAM FLOUR • RAPESEED OIL FOR SHALLOW-FRYING

LEMON SAUCE 4 TABLESPOONS NATURAL YOGURT (DAIRY OR VEGAN) • 4 TABLESPOONS GOOD-QUALITY MAYONNAISE (DAIRY OR VEGAN) • GRATED RIND OF ½ LEMON • 1–2 TABLESPOONS LEMON JUICE • WARM HALVED PITTA BREAD, SHREDDED LETTUCE, SLICED TOMATO, CUCUMBER AND ONION, MINT SPRIGS AND GRATED CARROT (OPTIONAL), TO SERVE

1 Put the chickpeas in a saucepan and cover with lots of water. Bring to the boil and boil for 2 minutes, then leave to soak for 1–2 hours. (Alternatively, just soak them overnight.) Drain.

2 Put the drained chickpeas into a food processor with the onion, coriander, garlic, cumin, bicarbonate of soda and salt and whiz until the ingredients are finely ground and hold together.

3 Take a small handful of the mixture and squeeze it between your palms to extract any excess liquid. Repeat until you've used up all the mixture, then coat the falafels lightly in flour.

4 Shallow-fry the falafel in hot rapeseed oil until brown and crisp on all sides. Drain on kitchen paper.

5 To make the sauce, simply mix all the ingredients together. Serve the falafel with the warm pitta bread: people can fill the pitta halves with a selection of hot falafels, salad and lemon sauce.

I generally use canned pulses for speed when cooking, but this is one recipe where you need to use dried ones for an authentic result.

Chilli kulfi

PREPARATION 15 MINUTES, PLUS STANDING AND FREEZING COOKING 5 MINUTES SERVES 4

750ml (1¼ pints) SINGLE CREAM • ¼ TEASPOON DRIED RED CHILLI FLAKES • 10 CARDAMOM PODS, CRUSHED •

A GOOD PINCH OF SAFFRON THREADS (OPTIONAL) • 175g (6oz) CASTER SUGAR • 2 TEASPOONS ROSEWATER

• 25g (1oz) GROUND ALMONDS • 25g (1oz) CHOPPED PISTACHIO NUTS • A FEW FRESH ROSE PETALS OR EXTRA

PISTACHIOS, TO DECORATE

1 Put the single cream into a saucepan with the chilli flakes, cardamom pods and saffron, if using. Bring to the boil, then remove from the heat, cover and leave for 10–15 minutes for the flavours to infuse.

2 Strain the mixture into a bowl and add the caster sugar, stirring until it dissolves. Stir in the rosewater, ground almonds and pistachio nuts and leave to cool.

3 Line 4 x 150ml (¼ pint) individual pudding basins, ramekins or disposable cups with clingfilm, then pour in the cooled kulfi mixture, dividing it evenly between them, and freeze until solid.

4 Remove the kulfi from the freezer about 15 minutes before you want to serve them. Turn them out of the containers on to dishes, peel off the clingfilm and serve, scattered with a few fresh rose petals if available or extra pistachios.

Espresso risotto

PREPARATION 10 MINUTES, PLUS STANDING COOKING 35–40 MINUTES SERVES 4

125g (4oz) RISOTTO OR PUDDING RICE • 150ml (¼ pint) WATER • 1 TABLESPOON GOOD-QUALITY STRONG INSTANT COFFEE GRANULES • 600ml (1 pint) SOYA MILK • 25g (1oz) UNSALTED BUTTER • 2 TABLESPOONS RUM • 150ml (¼ pint) DOUBLE CREAM, LIGHTLY WHIPPED • 1–2 TABLESPOONS COFFEE SUGAR CRYSTALS, TO DECORATE (OPTIONAL)

1 Put the rice and water into a medium-sized saucepan, bring to the boil and simmer for 5 minutes.

2 Add the coffee granules and the soya milk. Bring to the boil, then allow to boil away gently for 20–30 minutes, stirring frequently, until the rice is tender and the mixture quite thick.

3 Remove from the heat, add the unsalted butter and rum, cover and leave to stand for 10 minutes, or until ready to serve.

4 Serve into warmed individual bowls, top each with a generous spoonful of whipped double cream and a scattering of coffee sugar granules – or hand the cream and the sugar separately.

Soya milk is healthy for us and it gives a very creamy flavour to this risotto as well as to sauces. This is also good cold, with the whipped cream folded in.

Honey and ginger pashka with bitter chocolate sauce

PREPARATION 10 MINUTES, PLUS OVERNIGHT STANDING COOKING 5 MINUTES SERVES 4

50g (2oz) UNSALTED BUTTER, SOFTENED • 4 TABLESPOONS THICK HONEY • 500g (1lb) RICOTTA CHEESE •

GRATED RIND OF 1 ORANGE AND 1 LEMON • ½ TEASPOON VANILLA EXTRACT • 50g (2oz) CANDIED ORANGE

OR LEMON PEEL, CHOPPED • 50g (2oz) PRESERVED GINGER IN SYRUP, DRAINED AND CHOPPED •

50g (2oz) TOASTED FLAKED ALMONDS • A FEW EDIBLE FRESH FLOWERS, TO DECORATE (OPTIONAL)

SAUCE 100g (3½oz) BITTER CHOCOLATE, BROKEN INTO PIECES • 75ml (3fl oz) WATER

1 Prepare a clean plastic flowerpot, measuring 15cm (6 inches) across the top, by lining the inside with pieces of kitchen paper.

2 Put the unsalted butter into a food processor or large bowl with 2 tablespoons of the sugar, the ricotta, citrus rinds and vanilla and blend together, then stir in the candied peel, ginger and half the flaked almonds.

3 Spoon the mixture into the flowerpot and level the top. Stand the flowerpot in a bowl – to catch the liquid that will leak out – and leave in the refrigerator for 12–24 hours.

4 Just before you want to serve the pashka, make the sauce by melting together the chocolate and the water in a small saucepan over a gentle heat.

5 To serve, invert the flowerpot over a plate – the pashka will slide out easily and you can then peel off the paper. Quickly heat the remaining honey in a small saucepan and pour over the top of the pashka to make a glaze, which will run down the sides. Top with the remaining almonds and decorate the base with a few fresh flowers, if you like. Serve with the chocolate sauce in a small jug or bowl.

Coconut and honey ice cream with banana–sesame fritters

PREPARATION 10 MINUTES, PLUS FREEZING COOKING 35 MINUTES SERVES 4

400ml (14fl oz) CAN COCONUT MILK (SEE PAGE 41) • 3 TABLESPOONS THICK HONEY •

300ml (½ pint) DOUBLE CREAM

BANANA FRITTERS 125g (4oz) SELF-RAISING FLOUR • 2 TEASPOONS CASTER SUGAR • 175ml (6fl oz) WATER •

RAPESEED OIL FOR DEEP- OR SHALLOW-FRYING • 2 LARGE BANANAS, PEELED AND CUT INTO 1cm (½ inch)

DIAGONAL SLICES • 25g (1oz) SESAME SEEDS • LIME WEDGES, TO SERVE

1 First make the ice cream. Put the coconut milk into a bowl and whisk to remove lumps, then whisk in the honey and double cream. Pour into a suitable container and freeze until firm, removing it from the freezer and whisking it a couple of times during the freezing process. Alternatively, freeze in an ice-cream maker, following the manufacturer's instructions.

2 Take the ice cream out of the freezer 30 minutes or so before you want to serve it to allow it to soften a little.

3 To prepare the fritters, put the self-raising flour and caster sugar into a bowl and gradually stir in the water to make a coating batter.

4 Heat the rapeseed oil in a deep-fryer until a few drops of the batter when added to the pan sizzle and rise immediately to the surface of the oil. Dip slices of banana in the batter and slide into the hot oil – don't do too many at a time. Fry until the batter is crisp and golden brown, then remove the fritters with a slotted spoon, drain on kitchen paper and scatter with the sesame seeds.

5 Continue until all the fritters are done, then serve immediately, garnished with wedges of lime and accompanied by scoops of the coconut ice cream.

AL FRESCO

I love al fresco eating. From the first
warm spring day to the latest of the late
summer days, I'm outside. And whether
it's food cooked on a barbecue, made
indoors and taken out, or packed and
carried as a picnic, there's no doubt that
eating in the fresh air makes it all taste
extra special.

The food doesn't have to be complicated
– that's part of the joy – just well
flavoured and plentiful, like the recipes
in this section. They're for all kinds of
al fresco eating – from brunches to
barbecues, picnics to parties, finger foods
to fork buffets. So, come on sunshine!

Toasted Camembert open baguettes with shallots, thyme and redcurrants

PREPARATION 20 MINUTES COOKING 30 MINUTES SERVES 4

2 TABLESPOONS OLIVE OIL • 250g (8oz) SHALLOTS, SLICED • 4 THYME SPRIGS • 125g (4oz) REDCURRANTS •
1 TABLESPOON WATER • 125g (4oz) CASTER SUGAR • 2 SHORT BAGUETTES • 250g (8oz) CAMEMBERT CHEESE,
SLICED WITH RIND • LEAFY SALAD, TO SERVE

1 Heat 1 tablespoon of the olive oil in a saucepan. Add the shallots and thyme, cover and leave to cook gently for 10–15 minutes, until tender.

2 To make the sauce, put the redcurrants into a saucepan with the water and cook for 2–3 minutes, until the juices run. Add the caster sugar, bring to the boil and simmer for 5 minutes, then remove from the heat.

3 Split each baguette lengthways, then cut each length in half, to give 8 pieces in all. Scoop out most of the soft crumb – this will not be needed.

4 Place the baguettes on to a grill pan. Put a layer of shallots, with the thyme if you like, into each baguette, then top with slices of Camembert. Put a little of the redcurrant mixture along the top – you won't need it all.

5 Brush the edges of each baguette with the remaining oil, then put them under a preheated grill for 5–10 minutes, or until the bread has crisped and the Camembert has melted and become golden brown in places. Serve at once, with a leafy salad.

If you prefer, use good-quality redcurrant jelly (or cranberry sauce) instead of the fresh redcurrants.

Sage, onion and apple sausages

PREPARATION 15 MINUTES COOKING 20 MINUTES SERVES 4

2 TABLESPOONS OLIVE OIL, PLUS EXTRA FOR COOKING • 2 ONIONS, CHOPPED • 125g (4oz) STALE WHITE BREAD, TORN INTO CHUNKS • 10–12 SAGE LEAVES • 125g (4oz) CHEDDAR CHEESE, BROKEN INTO ROUGH CHUNKS • 125g (4oz) PEELED AND CORED SWEET EATING APPLE, CUT INTO CHUNKS • SALT AND PEPPER

1 Heat the olive oil in a pan, add the onions and fry for 10 minutes, until soft, then put them into a food processor with the bread, sage, Cheddar, apple and some salt and pepper to taste. Whiz until everything is chopped and starts to combine.

2 Check the seasoning, adding more salt and particularly pepper if required. Divide the mixture into 12 pieces and form each into a fat sausage shape, pressing the mixture together well.

3 Brush the 'sausages' with oil and grill, cook on the barbecue or shallow-fry them in a little oil, turning them so that they become golden brown all over. Drain on kitchen paper and eat while hot.

You can cook these sausages under a hot grill or on a barbecue; or you can shallow-fry them if you prefer.

142 – ROSE ELLIOT VEGETARIAN SUPERCOOK

Spicy bean cakes with lemon mayonnaise

PREPARATION 20 MINUTES COOKING 30–35 MINUTES SERVES 4

LEMON MAYONNAISE • I EGG • I TEASPOON DIJON MUSTARD • I TABLESPOON FRESHLY SQUEEZED
LEMON JUICE • 300ml (½ pint) VERY LIGHT OLIVE OIL OR OTHER NEUTRAL-TASTING OIL • SALT AND PEPPER
BEAN CAKES I TABLESPOON OLIVE OIL • I ONION, FINELY CHOPPED • I RED PEPPER, CORED, DESEEDED
AND CHOPPED • 2 GARLIC CLOVES, FINELY CHOPPED • I TEASPOON CUMIN SEEDS • ¼–½ TEASPOON
DRIED RED CHILLI FLAKES • 2 X 410g (13½oz) CANS BLACK BEANS OR RED KIDNEY BEANS, WELL DRAINED •
4 TABLESPOONS ROUGHLY CHOPPED CORIANDER • 2 TABLESPOONS LEMON MAYONNAISE (SEE ABOVE) •
50g (2oz) SOFT BREADCRUMBS • A LITTLE DRY POLENTA OR DRIED BREADCRUMBS FOR COATING • RAPESEED
OR LIGHT OLIVE OIL FOR SHALLOW-FRYING • LEMON WEDGES, TO SERVE

1 To make the mayonnaise, put the egg, mustard, lemon juice and salt and pepper into a food processor or blender and whiz for a few seconds to blend. Then, with the motor running, very slowly pour in the oil through the hole in the top of the mixer, barely a trickle at first, increasing as the mayonnaise thickens. It will be very thick when you have added all the oil. Check the seasoning and set aside.

2 To make the bean cakes, heat the olive oil in a saucepan, add the onion, cover and fry for 5 minutes. Then add the red pepper and garlic, stir, cover and cook for a further 10–15 minutes, until the vegetables are tender. Stir in the cumin seeds and chilli flakes, cook for a minute or two longer, then remove from the heat.

3 Add the beans to the onion mixture, breaking them up with a potato masher, or blitz them briefly in a food processor until they are coarsely mashed – it's nice to have some big pieces. Add the coriander and then stir in the mayonnaise and soft breadcrumbs, to make a soft mixture that holds together. Season with salt and pepper.

4 Divide the mixture into 8 equal pieces, dip into polenta or dried breadcrumbs and form into burger shapes. Shallow-fry in the rapeseed or olive oil on both sides until crisp – 2–3 minutes on each side. Drain on kitchen paper, then serve with the remaining lemon mayonnaise and some lemon wedges.

Baby potatoes and mushrooms on rosemary skewers

PREPARATION 15 MINUTES COOKING 25 MINUTES SERVES 4

18 BABY POTATOES • 6 ROSEMARY SPRIGS, 25–30cm (10–12 inches) LONG • 18 BABY CHESTNUT MUSHROOMS •

2–3 TABLESPOONS OLIVE OIL • MALDON SEA SALT FLAKES • LEMON MAYONNAISE (SEE PAGE 143), PEANUT DIP

(SEE PAGE 121) OR RED PEPPER HUMMUS (SEE PAGE 37), TO SERVE

1 Put the potatoes into a pan, cover with water and bring to the boil. Simmer until the potatoes are just tender when pierced with the point of a knife – about 6–10 minutes, depending on size. Drain and cool.

2 Using your fingers, pull off most of the leaves from the rosemary, leaving about 7–10cm (3–4 inches) at the top.

3 Thread the mushrooms and potatoes alternately on to the rosemary sprigs – they should go on easily. Brush all over with olive oil.

4 Put the skewers on to a preheated barbecue or under a preheated hot grill, keeping the leafy ends away from the heat, and cook for about 15 minutes, until the potatoes are golden brown and the mushrooms tender. Sprinkle with sea salt and serve with lemon mayonnaise, peanut dip or red pepper hummus.

If you can't get baby potatoes, use ordinary 'new' ones halved; and instead of rosemary sprigs, you could use wooden skewers.

Crispy nut balls coated in polenta

PREPARATION 20 MINUTES COOKING 20 MINUTES MAKES 24

75g (3oz) BUTTER • 2 GARLIC CLOVES, CRUSHED • I SMALL ONION, FINELY CHOPPED • 25g (1oz) FINE
WHOLEMEAL FLOUR • 200ml (7fl oz) SOYA MILK • 2 TEASPOONS CHOPPED OREGANO • 50g (2oz) HAZELNUTS,
FINELY GROUND • I EGG, BEATEN • DRY POLENTA FOR COATING • RAPESEED OIL FOR DEEP-FRYING •
SALT AND PEPPER • LEMON WEDGES, TO SERVE

1 Beat 50g (2oz) of the butter with the garlic until light and creamy, then form into a small block, wrap in foil and put into the refrigerator to chill and harden – this can be done well in advance if convenient.

2 Next, make the nut mixture, which also needs to be done in advance, so it can cool before use. Melt the remaining butter in a large saucepan, add the onion, cover and fry gently for about 7 minutes, until tender. Stir in the wholemeal flour and cook for 2–3 minutes, but don't let it brown, then pour in the soya milk and stir over the heat until very thick. Remove from the heat, stir in the oregano, ground hazelnuts and salt and pepper to taste. Spread out on a plate and leave to get completely cold.

3 Divide the firm garlic butter into 24 pieces. Take a heaped teaspoon of the nut mixture, form it into a small ball then push a piece of garlic butter into the centre and cover over with the nut mixture. Dip into beaten egg, then into the polenta. Continue until you've used all the butter and nut mixture and made 24 balls.

4 Heat the rapeseed oil to 180°C (350°F) or until a cube of bread immediately rises to the surface and browns in 30 seconds. Add the nut balls, a few at a time, and fry for a minute or two until golden brown and crisp. Drain on kitchen paper.

5 Put the nut balls on a serving plate and serve as they are with cocktail sticks and lemon wedges, or with a bowl of soy sauce dip (see page 150) or mayonnaise.

The nut mixture is moulded around a piece of garlic butter, giving a gorgeous burst of flavour as you bite into each ball. They're nice served with cocktail sticks and dipped into a sauce – either mayonnaise, if you feel like something rich and creamy, or a Japanese-style soy sauce dip for a clean, savoury flavour.

Japanese layered-omelette slices with dipping sauce

PREPARATION 20 MINUTES COOKING 15 MINUTES SERVES 4

8 EGGS • 8 TEASPOONS SOY SAUCE • 8 TABLESPOONS WATER • 4 TEASPOONS RAPESEED OIL FOR FRYING

• 2–3 TEASPOONS SESAME SEEDS, PAN-TOASTED • SPRING ONION CURLS (OPTIONAL), TO GARNISH

SOY SAUCE DIP 2 TABLESPOONS SOY SAUCE • 2 TABLESPOONS MIRIN • 2 TABLESPOONS SAKE

1 To prepare the dip, mix together the soy sauce, mirin and sake; put in a small serving bowl and set aside.

2 The quantities given are for 4 omelettes, which when sliced make about 32 pieces. You could make up the mixture for the whole quantity at once, but I think it's easier if you make just enough for one omelette at a time, as follows.

3 Whisk 2 eggs with 2 teaspoons of the soy sauce and 2 tablespoons of the water. Brush the frying pan with 1 teaspoon of the rapeseed oil and heat. Pour in 2–3 tablespoons of the beaten egg and tip the pan so that the egg covers the whole of the base. It will start to set immediately, so be ready to loosen the omelette with a fish slice or spatula and roll it up quite tightly.

4 Push the omelette right to the edge of the pan and pour in another 2–3 tablespoons of the egg mixture, letting it flow to the edges of the frying pan and up to and around the rolled-up omelette. When it sets, roll the rolled-up omelette over it, reroll and again push the roll to the edge of the pan.

5 Add more egg and make another omelette in the same way, until you have used all the first batch of egg and have quite a fat omelette. Take it out of the pan, place on a piece of foil and wrap up firmly, to help the layers to stick together. Make three more fat layered omelettes in the same way, adding 1 teaspoon of rapeseed oil to the pan for each one.

6 When you're ready to serve them – they can be served warm or cold – unwrap the omelettes and cut into 1cm (½ inch) slices. Arrange on a flat serving dish with the dip in the centre. Scatter with sesame seeds and garnish with spring onion curls, if you like.

This classic Japanese dish, called Tamago, is ideal for brunch or as an unusual nibble for a party.

Eggy tomatoes with garlic and basil

PREPARATION 10 MINUTES COOKING 15 MINUTES SERVES 4

4 BEEFSTEAK TOMATOES • 2 TABLESPOONS MILK OR CREAM • 8 EGGS, BEATEN • 50g (2oz) BUTTER •

1 GARLIC CLOVE, CRUSHED • 8 LARGE BASIL LEAVES, SHREDDED • SALT AND PEPPER • BUTTERED GRANARY

TOAST, TO SERVE

1 Cut the tomatoes in half horizontally and scoop out the seeds and pulp with a teaspoon. You won't need them for this recipe, but could add them to a soup or casserole – or just eat them!

2 Season the insides of the tomatoes with salt and pepper and put them, cut-side up, in a shallow gratin dish that will fit under your grill and that you can later take to the table. Cook under a preheated grill for about 10 minutes, or until tender, but not collapsed.

3 Just before the tomatoes are ready, prepare the scrambled eggs. Whisk the milk or cream into the beaten eggs and season with salt and pepper.

4 Cut half the butter into tiny pieces and set aside. Melt the remaining butter in a saucepan, add the garlic and cook for a few seconds, but don't let the butter or garlic brown.

5 Pour in the eggs and stir over a gentle heat until the eggs begin to thicken and scramble. As soon as this starts to happen, stir in the remaining butter and the basil and remove the pan from the heat – the eggs will continue to cook in the residual heat.

6 Spoon the scrambled egg into the tomato halves, dividing the mixture equally among them and serve immediately, with hot granary toast.

Grilled polenta with roasted tomatoes

PREPARATION 15 MINUTES COOKING 50 MINUTES SERVES 4

1.2 litres (2 pints) WATER • 250g (8oz) DRY POLENTA • 125g (4oz) PARMESAN CHEESE OR STRONG CHEDDAR CHEESE, GRATED • OLIVE OIL FOR BRUSHING • SALT AND PEPPER
ROASTED TOMATOES 1.1kg (2¼lb) TOMATOES ON THE VINE • 2 TABLESPOONS OLIVE OIL • 2 TABLESPOONS BALSAMIC VINEGAR • 8–10 THYME SPRIGS

1 To make the polenta, bring the water to the boil in a large saucepan. Add the polenta to the water in a thin steady stream, stirring all the time. Let it simmer for 5–10 minutes, stirring from time to time, or until it's very thick and leaves the sides of the pan.

2 Remove from the heat and stir in the Parmesan or Cheddar and salt and pepper to taste. Turn the mixture on to a lightly oiled baking sheet or large plate and spread and press it out to a depth of 5–7mm (¼–⅓ inch). Leave to become completely cold and firm.

3 To roast the tomatoes, put them, complete with their vines, into a roasting tin. Drizzle with the olive oil and vinegar, scatter with a little salt and the thyme sprigs and place in the top of a preheated oven, 200°C (400°F), Gas Mark 6, for 40–45 minutes.

4 Just before you want to serve the meal, cut the polenta into manageable pieces, brush lightly with olive oil and cook under a preheated grill on both sides, until crisp and lightly charred. Serve at once, with the tomatoes.

You can vary the flavouring for the polenta – try using chopped, pitted black or green olives instead of the cheese or just lots of chopped thyme and oregano.

Stilton pâté with roasted baby beetroots, dill and chicory salad

PREPARATION 15 MINUTES COOKING 1–1½ HOURS SERVES 4

450g (14½oz) BABY BEETROOTS, PREFERABLY NO BIGGER THAN PLUMS • OLIVE OIL FOR RUBBING
• DILL SPRIGS AND COARSELY GROUND BLACK PEPPER, TO GARNISH • RUSTIC BREAD, TO SERVE
STILTON PÂTÉ 200g (7oz) LOW-FAT SOFT CREAM CHEESE • 1 TEASPOON DIJON MUSTARD • 200g (7oz) STILTON
CHEESE, ROUGHLY CRUMBLED • 1 TABLESPOON VEGETARIAN PORT OR SWEET SHERRY • PEPPER
SALAD 2–3 CHICORY • 1 BUNCH OF WATERCRESS • 50g (2oz) WALNUTS

1 If the beetroots still have leaves attached, cut these off about 5cm (2 inches) from the beetroot. Scrub the beetroots gently, being careful not to pierce the skin, and leave the long 'tail' on, if still attached. Rub the beetroots with a little olive oil, wrap them lightly in a piece of foil and bake in a preheated oven, 200°C (400°F), Gas Mark 6, for 1–1½ hours, or until tender right through when pierced with a knife. You could uncover them for the last 30 minutes or so, but you don't want them to get too crisp. I like to eat them skins and all, but most people rub off the skins before eating.

2 While the beetroot is cooking, prepare the pâté. Whiz the cream cheese, mustard, Stilton and port or sherry to a cream in a food processor. Season with a little pepper.

3 Mix the ingredients for the salad together.

4 To serve, put a spoonful of the Stilton pâté on each plate with some of the beetroot – baby ones can be left whole, larger ones cut as necessary – and one or two feathery leaves of dill. Coarsely grind some black pepper over the top and serve with the salad and rustic bread.

Lentil and olive pâté with grilled fennel

PREPARATION 10 MINUTES COOKING 10 MINUTES SERVES 4

4 FENNEL BULBS • 2 TABLESPOONS OLIVE OIL • SALT AND PEPPER • LEMON WEDGES, TO SERVE

PÂTÉ 2 GARLIC CLOVES • 410g (13½oz) CAN GREEN LENTILS, DRAINED • 150g (5oz) BLACK OLIVES,

SUCH AS KALAMATA, PITTED

1 Trim the tops off the fennel, then, using a sharp knife or a potato peeler, shave off a thin layer of the outer bracts, to remove any tough threads. Cut the bulbs in half, then into quarters or sixths, depending on the size of the fennel. Brush the pieces on both sides with olive oil, place on a grill pan and grill under a preheated very hot grill for about 10 minutes, or until tender and browned, turning them as necessary.

2 Meanwhile, make the pâté. Put the garlic cloves into a food processor and whiz to chop, then add the lentils and black olives and whiz again to a thick, fairly chunky consistency.

3 Heap the pâté up on a plate, arrange the grilled fennel and lemon wedges around the edge and serve.

Cheese and sun-blush tomato muffins

PREPARATION 10 MINUTES COOKING 20 MINUTES MAKES 9

225g (7½oz) PLAIN COTTAGE CHEESE • 65g (2½oz) PARMESAN CHEESE, FRESHLY GRATED • 50g (2oz) SOYA FLOUR
• 100g (3½oz) GROUND ALMONDS • 1 TEASPOON BAKING POWDER • 8 SUN-BLUSH TOMATO PIECES, FINELY
CHOPPED • 4 TABLESPOONS CHOPPED BASIL • 4 TABLESPOONS WATER • 4 EGGS • SALT AND PEPPER

1 Line a 9-hole muffin tin with medium-sized muffin cases (like cup-cake cases).

2 Put the cottage cheese into a bowl with all but 15g (½oz) of the Parmesan, the soya flour, ground almonds, baking powder, sun-blush tomatoes, basil, water and eggs and season with salt and pepper, then mix all together.

3 Spoon the mixture into the muffin cases, scatter with the remaining Parmesan and bake in a preheated oven, 200°C (400°F), Gas Mark 6, for 20 minutes, or until set, risen and golden brown. Serve as soon as possible – they're lovely eaten warm.

Everyone enjoys these light, puffy, protein-rich savoury muffins – and as they don't contain any wheat flour, they're ideal for people who are watching their carbohydrate intake.

Haloumi with lime vinaigrette and mint in toasted mini pitta

PREPARATION 10 MINUTES COOKING 10 MINUTES SERVES 4

GRATED RIND AND JUICE OF 2 LIMES • 4 TABLESPOONS OLIVE OIL • 500g (1lb) HALOUMI CHEESE •

8 MINI PITTA BREADS • LEAVES FROM 1 BUNCH OF MINT, ROUGHLY CHOPPED • ½ CUCUMBER, THINLY

SLICED LENGTHWAYS • SALT AND PEPPER

1 First make a lime vinaigrette by whisking together the rind and juice of the limes, the olive oil and some pepper – don't add any salt at this point because the haloumi cheese may supply enough. Set aside.

2 Drain off any water from the haloumi and blot the cheese with kitchen paper if necessary. Cut the haloumi into slices about 5mm (¼ inch) thick and put them in a single layer in an unoiled frying pan. Fry over a moderate to hot heat until they are browned on one side – this will take only a minute or two – then flip them over and cook the other side.

3 While the haloumi is cooking, toast the pitta breads under the grill.

4 Remove the slices of haloumi from the pan when cooked and arrange them in a shallow serving dish. Pour over the lime vinaigrette and scatter with the mint, making sure that each slice gets coated. Serve with the toasted pitta and sliced cucumber.

This is very fresh-tasting and can be prepared in advance. I find it a very useful standby for unexpected visitors because it's easy to make and packets of haloumi keep for a long time in the refrigerator.

Honeydew melon, strawberry and mint compôte

PREPARATION 15 MINUTES, PLUS STANDING SERVES 4

20g (¾oz) MINT LEAVES • 75g (3oz) CASTER SUGAR OR CLEAR HONEY • 1 RIPE HONEYDEW MELON •

500g (1lb) STRAWBERRIES, HULLED AND SLICED

1 Put the mint leaves into a large bowl and crush lightly with the end of a rolling pin or a wooden spoon. Add the caster sugar or honey and crush the leaves again by pressing them against the side of the bowl with a wooden spoon. Set aside.

2 Halve the melon, scoop out and discard the seeds. Scoop out the flesh with a melon-baller, or simply use a sharp knife to cut it away from the skin and into bite-sized pieces.

3 Put the melon into a bowl with the mint and add the strawberries. Stir, then cover and leave for 1–4 hours for the flavours to blend. The fruit compôte will produce its own liquid and is deliciously refreshing served cold, but not icy.

You can't tell by its scent whether a honeydew melon is ripe so buy from a reputable supplier in July or August to be sure of one with succulent, sweet and melting flesh.

Spicy vegan carrot cake

PREPARATION 20 MINUTES COOKING 1¼ HOURS SERVES 4

250g (8oz) SCRAPED CARROTS, GRATED • 125g (4oz) RAISINS • 6 TABLESPOONS RAPESEED OR OLIVE OIL • 125g (4oz) UNREFINED CANE SUGAR • 250g (8oz) SELF-RAISING FLOUR • 1 TEASPOON GRATED NUTMEG • 1 TEASPOON GROUND CINNAMON • 8 TABLESPOONS APPLE JUICE CONCENTRATE (AVAILABLE FROM HEALTH FOOD SHOPS) OR REAL MAPLE SYRUP • 4 TABLESPOONS ORANGE JUICE FROSTING 200g (7oz) DAIRY-FREE ALTERNATIVE TO SOFT CHEESE • GRATED RIND OF 1 ORANGE • 25g (1oz) CASTER SUGAR • STRANDS OF ORANGE RIND, TO DECORATE

1 Line a 20cm (8 inch) square cake tin with nonstick baking paper.

2 Put the carrots, raisins, rapeseed or olive oil and sugar into a bowl and mix. Then add the flour, nutmeg, cinnamon, apple and orange juices and mix again until everything is combined – the mixture will be quite sticky.

3 Spoon into the prepared cake tin, level the top, and bake in a preheated oven, 160°C (325°F), Gas Mark 3, for 1¼ hours, or until a skewer inserted into the centre comes out clean. Leave in the tin until completely cold.

4 To make the frosting, mix the dairy-free alternative to soft cheese with the orange rind and caster sugar, then spread over the top of the cold cake. Decorate with strands of orange rind.

Grilled pineapple with palm sugar and crème fraîche

PREPARATION 10 MINUTES COOKING 10 MINUTES SERVES 4

I LARGE RIPE JUICY PINEAPPLE • NEUTRAL COOKING OIL SUCH AS RAPESEED OR LIGHT OLIVE OIL FOR BRUSHING • 300ml (½ pint) CRÈME FRAÎCHE • 175g (6oz) PALM SUGAR, CHOPPED IF IN A SOLID BLOCK

1 Cut the pineapple lengthways through the leaves, first in half, then into sixths or eighths, depending on the size of the pineapple – it's best if the wedges are no more than about 1cm (½ inch) thick. Brush them all over with the cooking oil.

2 Put the pineapple slices on a grill pan and cook under a preheated grill, or lay them directly on the grid of a barbecue. Cook for about 10 minutes in all, turning them halfway through cooking when the first side is tender and, if on a grid, attractively marked by it. Remove from the heat and sprinkle with palm sugar.

3 Serve the pineapple with bowls of the crème fraîche and palm sugar for people to help themselves.

The pineapple can be cooked under a hot grill, but the very nicest way to do it is on a barbecue at the end of the main cooking, when the embers are dying down – it makes a lovely end to an al fresco meal.

Waffles with black cherry sauce and soured cream

PREPARATION 15 MINUTES COOKING 20 MINUTES SERVES 4

175g (6oz) PLAIN FLOUR • 1 TEASPOON BAKING POWDER • ½ TEASPOON SALT • 4 TEASPOONS CASTER

SUGAR • 2 TABLESPOONS OLIVE OIL • 2 EGGS • 250ml (8fl oz) MILK • 25–50g (1–2oz) BUTTER, MELTED •

300ml (½ pint) SOURED CREAM AND CASTER SUGAR, TO SERVE

CHERRY SAUCE 1kg (2lb) BLACK CHERRIES, PITTED • 150ml (¼ pint) WATER, PLUS 1–2 TABLESPOONS •

2 TEASPOONS CORNFLOUR • 4 TABLESPOONS CASTER SUGAR

1 First make the cherry sauce. Put the cherries into a saucepan with the 150ml (¼ pint) water. Bring to the boil, then cover and simmer gently for about 5 minutes, or until the cherries are tender.

2 Mix the cornflour with the 1–2 tablespoons cold water, then add to the cherries, bring to the boil and stir for a minute or two until the sauce is slightly thickened. Stir in the caster sugar and remove from the heat. Set aside.

3 To make the batter for the waffles or pancakes, put the flour, baking powder, salt and caster sugar into a bowl. Make a well in the centre, add the olive oil and break in the eggs. Beat with a wooden spoon or whisk, then add a little of the milk to loosen the mixture. Continue whisking and adding milk until you have a batter about the consistency of unwhipped double cream, adding a little more flour or milk as required to achieve this. Cover the batter and set aside until required.

4 Make waffles using a waffle iron following the manufacturer's instructions, using the melted butter to grease the iron as necessary. Alternatively, to make pancakes, heat a frying pan and swirl in about 1 teaspoon of melted butter. When the frying pan is hot enough to sizzle when a drop of water is flicked into it, pour in 2–3 tablespoons of batter. Tip the pan so that the batter runs all over the surface. After a few seconds, when the pancake has set, loosen it with a fish slice and flip it over to cook the other side. Then lift it out on to a plate. Continue with the remaining batter, piling the pancakes up on top of each other.

5 Serve the waffles or pancakes with the cherry sauce (hot, warm or cold, as you wish), the soured cream and some caster sugar sprinkled on top.

This combination is gorgeous, but if you haven't got a waffle iron, you can make pancakes instead, as I've explained in the recipe. A cherry stoner is useful for pitting the cherries – an inexpensive gadget that's surprisingly useful.

CELEBRATIONS

Food plays an important part in festivals and celebrations and here are some spectacular recipes to add some real pizzazz. There's a gorgeous *Ricotta 'cake' with honey- and cardamom-roasted vegetables* for summer, a *Wild mushroom roulade* for autumn and a *Moroccan-flavoured aubergine Wellington* for Thanksgiving.

The *Christmas galette* is packed with all the traditional flavours and my family's favourite, *Whole baked Brie in filo with apricot sauce,* turns any day into a celebration. And puddings aren't forgotten: who could resist *Dreamy raspberry and rose pavlova*, the queen of puddings?

Red lentil and roasted pepper soup

PREPARATION 20 MINUTES COOKING 40 MINUTES SERVES 6

2 RED ONIONS, CUT INTO 2.5cm (1 inch) PIECES • 2 TEASPOONS OLIVE OIL • 2 RED PEPPERS, HALVED, CORED AND DESEEDED • 4 GARLIC CLOVES, UNPEELED • SMALL HANDFUL OF THYME • 125g (4oz) SPLIT RED LENTILS • 600ml (1 pint) WATER • 2 BAY LEAVES • SALT AND PEPPER • CHOPPED BASIL AND A FEW SHAVINGS OF PARMESAN CHEESE, TO SERVE

1 Toss the onions in the olive oil and put them on a baking sheet, along with the peppers, which don't need oiling. Roast in a preheated oven, 180°C (350°F), Gas Mark 4, for 30 minutes, or until the vegetables are nearly tender, then add the garlic and thyme to the baking sheet and cook for 10 minutes more, until all the vegetables are tender. Set aside to cool.

2 Meanwhile, put the red lentils into a saucepan with the water and bay leaves. Bring to the boil, then simmer for 15 minutes, or until the lentils are soft and pale coloured. Remove and discard the bay leaves.

3 Rub off as much of the skin from the peppers as you can – get rid of any very dark bits, but don't worry about being too particular. Pop the garlic out of its skin with your fingers. Put the peppers and garlic into a food processor with the onion (discard the thyme). Add the lentils together with their cooking liquid and whiz to a smooth, creamy consistency, thinning it with a little water, if necessary.

4 Return the mixture to the pan and reheat gently. Season to taste with salt and pepper, then ladle into warmed bowls and top each with basil and thin shavings of Parmesan.

One of my favourites for entertaining, this is really delicious and makes a great centrepiece at any dinner party.

Wild mushroom roulade

PREPARATION 20 MINUTES COOKING 25 MINUTES SERVES 6

20g (¾oz) FLAT LEAF PARSLEY • 175g (6oz) LOW-FAT SOFT CREAM CHEESE • 175g (6oz) GRUYÈRE CHEESE,
FINELY GRATED • 4 EGGS, SEPARATED • SALT AND PEPPER • TOMATO SAUCE (SEE PAGE 128), TO SERVE
FILLING I TABLESPOON OLIVE OIL • 500g (1lb) MIXED WILD MUSHROOMS OR OYSTER MUSHROOMS, WIPED •
4 GARLIC CLOVES, FINELY CHOPPED • 150g (5oz) GARLIC AND HERB CREAM CHEESE • 1–2 TABLESPOONS
HOT WATER

1 Line a 23 x 33cm (9 x 13 inch) Swiss roll tin with nonstick baking paper so that it extends about 5cm (2 inches) on all sides.

2 Set aside half the parsley for the garnish. Chop the remainder and put into a large bowl with the low-fat cheese, the Gruyère and the egg yolks. Mix well and season with salt and pepper.

3 In another bowl, whisk the egg whites until they stand in stiff peaks, then, using a large metal spoon, fold them lightly into the Gruyère mixture.

4 Pour the mixture into the lined Swiss roll tin, spreading it evenly into the corners. Bake in a preheated oven, 200°C (400°F), Gas Mark 6, for 12 minutes or until firm, golden brown and well risen.

5 While the roulade is cooking, make the filling. Heat the oil in a large saucepan, add the mushrooms and garlic and fry over quite a high heat until the mushrooms are tender – 4–5 minutes. You can assemble the roulade at this point, or you can do it after the roulade has cooled when it can be a little easier to roll.

6 Put a large piece of nonstick paper, a little bigger than the roulade, on the work surface and turn out the cooked roulade on to it. Peel off the baking paper from the roulade.

7 Mix the garlic and herb cream cheese with enough hot water to soften it a little, then spread it evenly over the roulade. Arrange the mushrooms on top, taking them to within 1cm (½ inch) of the short edges. Make sure any thick mushroom stems are parallel with the short edges – this makes it easier to roll them up. Now for the fun! Starting with one short end, fold up about 1cm (½ inch) of the roulade and press it down firmly. Using the paper to help you and holding the folded end through the paper, start rolling firmly, then press the roulade into a good shape when it's rolled up.

8 Put the roulade, seam-side down, on to a heatproof serving plate. Now either reheat it in the oven for 5–10 minutes until piping hot, or let it go cold and reheat it later for 10–15 minutes. It will puff up a bit and smell divine.

9 Garnish the top with the remaining parsley and cut into thick slices to serve, with the tomato sauce.

Butternut squash with porcini and garlic stuffing and celeriac mash

PREPARATION 20 MINUTES COOKING 45 MINUTES SERVES 6

45g (SCANT 2oz) DRIED PORCINI MUSHROOMS • 6 FAT GARLIC CLOVES • 4 TABLESPOONS OLIVE OIL •

2 BUTTERNUT SQUASH • SALT AND PEPPER • FLAT LEAF PARSLEY SPRIGS, TO GARNISH

CELERIAC MASH 750g (1½lb) CELERIAC, CUT INTO EVEN-SIZED PIECES • 500g (1lb) POTATOES, PEELED AND CUT

INTO EVEN-SIZED PIECES • 2 TABLESPOONS OLIVE OIL

1 Put the porcini into a saucepan with water to cover, bring to the boil and boil for about 2 minutes, or until just tender. Drain – the liquid isn't needed for this recipe, but you could freeze it for later as it makes fantastic stock for soups and gravies.

2 Put the porcini into a food processor with the garlic, 3 tablespoons of the olive oil and a seasoning of salt and pepper and whiz to a coarse purée.

3 Cut the butternut squash in half lengthways, down through the stem. Scoop out the seeds with a teaspoon and discard. Rub the remaining olive oil and a little salt into the flesh, then fill the cavities with the porcini mixture, dividing it between all 4 of them.

4 Put the butternut squash halves, cut-side down, on to a baking sheet and bake in a preheated oven, 200°C (400°F), Gas Mark 6, for about 40 minutes, or until you can insert a sharp pointed knife easily into the skin and the flesh inside feels tender.

5 While the squash are cooking, make the celeriac mash. Put the celeriac and potatoes into a saucepan, cover with water and simmer for 15–20 minutes, or until tender. Drain, reserving the liquid (this, too, makes fabulous stock). Mash or purée in a food processor with the olive oil, salt and pepper and enough of the reserved liquid to make a soft, creamy consistency.

6 To serve, carefully lift the squash off the baking sheet, making sure that the stuffing doesn't get left behind. Cut each squash half in two and place on a serving dish – they look good arranged like the rays of the sun on a large flat round plate – and garnish with a few parsley sprigs. Serve the celeriac mash separately.

Whole baked Brie in filo with apricot sauce

PREPARATION 15 MINUTES, PLUS STANDING COOKING 30–40 MINUTES SERVES 6

2 X 275g (9oz) PACKETS FILO PASTRY • 50–75ml (2–3fl oz) OLIVE OIL • I WHOLE BRIE CHEESE, 20–25cm (8–10 inches) DIAMETER, FIRM AND UNDER-RIPE IF POSSIBLE • MASHED POTATO AND GREEN BEANS, TO SERVE

SAUCE 500g (1lb) JAR APRICOT CONSERVE • 4 TABLESPOONS LEMON JUICE

1 Take a sheet of filo pastry, place on a baking sheet large enough to hold the Brie and brush the pastry with olive oil. Place another sheet overlapping it, and brush with more oil. The idea is to make a square of filo that is big enough to form a base for the Brie and that can also be brought up the sides. It's better to have too large a square than too small because you will be trimming off excess pastry later.

2 Put the Brie on top of the filo, then cut the filo, allowing about 10cm (4 inches) all round the Brie. Now, build up more layers of filo on top of the Brie – this layer needs to cover the cheese with about 5cm (2 inches) to spare around the sides. Fold up the bottom layer of filo to meet the top layer and roll them together to secure them and form a decorative seal all round the Brie. Brush with more oil and make a steam hole in the middle.

3 You can scrunch up some of the filo trimmings or cut ribbons out of them, brush with oil and use to decorate the top of the pie in any way that takes your fancy. The pie will keep in a cool place for several hours.

4 When you're ready to bake the Brie, place it, on its baking sheet, into a preheated oven, 200°C (400°F), Gas Mark 6, and bake for 30–40 minutes, until the pastry is golden brown and crisp. Remove from the oven and let it stand for 10–15 minutes, to settle, then slide very carefully on to a large platter. It looks fantastic, but once cut the Brie will ooze all over the place, so make sure it's on a large enough platter, preferably with sides, or on a plate standing on a tray.

5 To make the apricot sauce, put the apricot conserve and the lemon juice into a small saucepan and bring to the boil. Pour into a jug to serve. Serve the mashed potato and green beans separately.

Christmas galette

PREPARATION 30 MINUTES, PLUS CHILLING COOKING 30–35 MINUTES SERVES 6

TART CASE 375g (12oz) FINE WHOLEMEAL FLOUR OR HALF WHOLEMEAL, HALF WHITE • 175g (6oz) BUTTER, CUT INTO ROUGH CHUNKS • ½ TEASPOON SALT • 3 TABLESPOONS COLD WATER • 2 TABLESPOONS OLIVE OIL

FILLING 375g (12oz) CARROTS, SCRAPED AND CUT INTO RINGS • 375g (12oz) LEEKS, TRIMMED AND CUT INTO 2.5cm (1 inch) PIECES • 275g (9 oz) SHALLOTS • 375g (12 oz) TRIMMED BABY BRUSSELS SPROUTS • 2 COX APPLES, PEELED, CORED AND CHOPPED • 100g (3½oz) CASHEW NUTS • SALT AND PEPPER • CHOPPED PARSLEY, TO GARNISH

SAUCE 50g (2 oz) BUTTER • 2 TABLESPOONS CORNFLOUR OR ARROWROOT • 200ml (7fl oz) SOYA MILK • 175g (6oz) STILTON CHEESE, CRUMBLED

1 To make the pastry, put the flour, butter and salt into a food processor and whiz until it resembles coarse breadcrumbs. Alternatively, put the ingredients in a bowl and rub the butter into the flour with your fingertips. Add the water and mix to a dough.

2 Turn out the dough on to a lightly floured surface. Knead briefly, then form into a circle and roll out to fit a round flan tin measuring 30cm (12 inches) across and 3.5cm (1½ inches) deep. Trim the edges, prick the base thoroughly all over, then chill for 30 minutes.

3 Bake the tart in a preheated oven, 200°C (400°F), Gas Mark 6, for 20 minutes, until the pastry is 'set' and lightly browned. A minute or two before you take it out of the oven, heat the olive oil in a small saucepan until smoking hot. As soon as the tart comes out of the oven, pour the hot olive oil all over the base – it will sizzle and almost 'fry'. This will 'waterproof' the base of the tart so that it will remain crisp.

4 To make the filling, half-fill a large saucepan with water and bring to the boil. Add the carrots, leeks and shallots, bring back to the boil, cover and cook for 5 minutes, then add the sprouts, cover and cook for a further 6–7 minutes, until all the vegetables are tender. Drain.

5 To make the sauce, melt the butter in a saucepan and stir in the cornflour or arrowroot. When it froths at the edges, pour in the soya milk and stir over the heat until it has thickened. Remove from the heat and stir in the Stilton. Season with salt and pepper.

6 Mix the sauce with the drained vegetables and the apple. Check the seasoning, then spoon into the tart case and top with the cashews. Put back into the oven for 10–15 minutes, until the filling is piping hot and the cashews are golden brown. Scatter with some parsley and serve at once.

This galette is full of Christmas flavours. Serve it with roast potatoes and cranberry sauce.

Artichoke and green olive 'cake' with sizzling pine nuts and saffron cream

PREPARATION 30 MINUTES COOKING 1¼ HOURS SERVES 6

25g (1oz) BUTTER, PLUS EXTRA FOR GREASING • 1 TABLESPOON OLIVE OIL • 500g (1lb) NEW POTATOES, CUT INTO 2.5mm (⅛ inch) SLICES • 150ml (¼ pint) WATER • 500g (1lb) COOKED ARTICHOKE BASES OR MARINATED HEARTS, ROUGHLY CHOPPED • 150g (5oz) LARGE GREEN OLIVES, PITTED AND ROUGHLY CHOPPED • 4 TABLESPOONS CHOPPED PARSLEY • 50g (2oz) SOFT WHITE BREADCRUMBS • 4 EGGS, BEATEN • 150ml (¼ pint) SINGLE CREAM • SALT AND PEPPER • FLAT LEAF PARSLEY, TO GARNISH SAFFRON CREAM 300ml (½ pint) DOUBLE CREAM • ½ TEASPOON SAFFRON THREADS TOPPING 25g (1oz) BUTTER • 1 TABLESPOON OLIVE OIL • 4 GARLIC CLOVES, SLICED • 2 TABLESPOONS PINE NUTS

1 Line a 1kg (2lb) loaf tin with a strip of nonstick baking paper and grease with butter.

2 Heat the butter and olive oil in a saucepan, then add the potatoes and water. Bring to the boil, then cover and cook gently for 10–15 minutes, or until the potatoes are tender and most of the water has gone.

3 Mix together the potatoes and their cooking liquid, the artichokes, olives, parsley, breadcrumbs, beaten eggs, single cream and salt and pepper to taste. Spoon the mixture into the prepared loaf tin and bake in a preheated oven, 180°C (350°F), Gas Mark 4, for 1 hour, or until it is firm and a skewer inserted into the centre comes out clean.

4 To make the saffron cream, put the double cream and saffron into a saucepan, bring to the boil, then season with salt and pepper. Leave to infuse until ready to serve, then reheat.

5 Turn out the 'cake' on to a warmed serving platter and keep warm while you prepare the pine nut topping. Heat the butter and olive oil in a saucepan and add the garlic and pine nuts. Cook over a moderate heat for a minute or two until the pine nuts and garlic are golden brown, then remove from the heat and pour, sizzling, over the top of the cake. Garnish with some flat leaf parsley and serve at once, with the saffron cream.

You can buy marinated artichoke hearts from a deli, use frozen bases or, for perfection, boil the bases of globe artichokes until tender, having first cut off all the leaves and removed the 'chokes'.

Moroccan-flavoured aubergine Wellington

PREPARATION 20 MINUTES COOKING I HOUR SERVES 6

125g (4oz) COUSCOUS • 2 TABLESPOONS OLIVE OIL • I ONION, CHOPPED • I AUBERGINE, CUT INTO
1cm (½ inch) CUBES • I RED PEPPER, CORED, DESEEDED AND CUT INTO 1cm (½ inch) PIECES • 25g (1oz)
READY-TO-EAT DRIED APRICOTS, CHOPPED • 25g (1oz) RAISINS • 2 GARLIC CLOVES, CRUSHED • I TABLESPOON
GROUND CINNAMON • I TABLESPOON GROUND CUMIN • I TABLESPOON CHOPPED MINT • I TABLESPOON
CHOPPED PARSLEY • 100g (3½oz) TOASTED FLAKED ALMONDS • 125g (4oz) PITTED BLACK OLIVES, SLICED •
2 X 350g (11½oz) SHEETS OF READY-ROLLED PUFF PASTRY • SOYA MILK FOR BRUSHING • SESAME SEEDS
FOR SPRINKLING • SALT AND PEPPER • MINT RAITA (SEE PAGE 125), TO SERVE

1 Put the couscous into a bowl, cover with boiling water and set aside to soak.

2 Heat the olive oil in a large saucepan, add the onion and fry for 5 minutes, then add the aubergine and pepper, cover and cook gently for 10–15 minutes, or until the vegetables are tender. Add the apricots, raisins, garlic, cinnamon and cumin and stir over the heat for a minute or two until the spices smell aromatic. Remove from the heat.

3 Drain the couscous thoroughly in a sieve and add it to the pan, along with the mint, parsley, almonds and olives. Season to taste with salt and pepper and leave the mixture to cool.

4 Spread one of the pastry sheets out on a baking sheet and brush with soya milk.

5 Put the aubergine mixture in the centre of the pastry. Place the second sheet of pastry over the top and press the edges together. Trim the edges, leaving a 2.5cm (1 inch) border. Pinch the edges with your fingers and thumbs. Brush with soya milk and sprinkle with sesame seeds.

6 Bake in a preheated oven, 200°C (400°F), Gas Mark 6, for 40 minutes, until the pastry has puffed up and is golden brown. Transfer to a warmed serving platter and serve at once with the mint raita.

Ricotta 'cake' with honey- and cardamom-roasted vegetables

PREPARATION 20 MINUTES COOKING 1 HOUR SERVES 6

1kg (2lb) RICOTTA CHEESE • 300g (10oz) PECORINO CHEESE, GRATED • 8 GARLIC CLOVES, CRUSHED •
GRATED NUTMEG • SEVERAL BASIL SPRIGS
ROASTED VEGETABLES 12 CARDAMOM PODS, LIGHTLY CRUSHED • 2 TABLESPOONS HONEY • 2 TABLESPOONS
OLIVE OIL • 2 RED PEPPERS, CORED, DESEEDED AND SLICED • 2 YELLOW PEPPERS, CORED, DESEEDED AND
SLICED • 2 LARGE COURGETTES, CUT INTO 5 X 1cm (2 X ½ inch) BATONS • 1 AUBERGINE, CUT INTO 5 X 1cm
(2 X ½ inch) BATONS • 4 RED ONIONS, CUT INTO WEDGES • SALT AND PEPPER

1 Start with the roasted vegetables. Mix the cardamom pods, honey, olive oil and some salt and pepper in a large bowl and add the peppers, courgettes, aubergine and onions. Mix the vegetables gently to coat them lightly in the oil, then spread them out in one or two roasting tins and place in a preheated oven, 190°C (375°F), Gas Mark 5. Bake for 50–60 minutes, stirring a couple of times, or until tender and lightly browned in places.

2 To make the ricotta cake, mix together the ricotta, 250g (8 oz) of the Pecorino and the garlic. Season to taste with salt, pepper and nutmeg.

3 Turn the mixture into a lightly greased 23cm (9 inch) round nonstick springform tin. Smooth the top, scatter with the remaining Pecorino and bake in the oven, with the vegetables, for 30 minutes, until firm in the centre and golden brown.

4 Remove the ricotta cake from the oven and leave to stand for 4–5 minutes, then slip a knife around the edges of the tin. Invert it on to a large serving dish and turn out the cake. Spoon the vegetables on top and around the cake, decorate with a few basil sprigs and serve immediately.

Luscious vegan pumpkin pie

PREPARATION 30 MINUTES, PLUS PUMPKIN BAKING COOKING 40 MINUTES SERVES 6

300g (10oz) FINE WHOLEMEAL FLOUR OR HALF WHOLEMEAL, HALF WHITE • 150g (5oz) BUTTER OR VEGAN MARGARINE, CUT INTO ROUGH CHUNKS • ½ TEASPOON SALT • 2–3 TABLESPOONS COLD WATER • 2–3 TABLESPOONS SOYA MILK • CASTER SUGAR FOR DREDGING • GROUND CINNAMON FOR SPRINKLING FILLING 500g (1lb) WELL-DRAINED COOKED, OR CANNED, PUMPKIN • 275g (9oz) FIRM TOFU, DRAINED, PATTED DRY AND BROKEN INTO CHUNKS • 125g (4oz) SOFT BROWN SUGAR • 1 TABLESPOON BLACK TREACLE • 1 TEASPOON GROUND CINNAMON • ½ TEASPOON GROUND GINGER • ½ TEASPOON GRATED NUTMEG

1 If you are using fresh pumpkin, small ones (or butternut squash) are best. Halve, deseed and place, cut-side down, on a baking sheet. Bake in a preheated oven, 200°C (400°F), Gas Mark 6, until tender – 40–60 minutes, depending on the size of the pumpkin.

2 Meanwhile, make the pastry. Put the flour, butter and salt into a food processor and whiz until it resembles coarse bread-crumbs. Alternatively, put the ingredients in a bowl and rub the butter into the flour with your fingertips. Add the water and mix to a dough.

3 Turn out the dough on to a lightly floured surface. Knead briefly, then form into a circle and roll out to fit a 23cm (9 inch) round flan dish. Trim the edges and reserve the trimmings.

4 To make the filling, remove the pumpkin skin if using fresh pumpkin and chop the flesh. Put the pumpkin into a food processor with the tofu, soft brown sugar, treacle and spices and whiz to a thick, smooth purée. Pour into the flan case and gently smooth the top.

5 Reroll the pastry trimmings, brush with soya milk, dredge with a little caster sugar and sprinkle with cinnamon. Cut into strips and arrange in a lattice on top of the pumpkin filling. As well as looking attractive, this topping will become crisp, contrasting with the soft filling and helping to hold it together.

6 Bake the pie in a preheated oven, 180°C (350°F), Gas Mark 4, for 40 minutes, until the filling is just set and the topping crisp. Serve hot, warm or cold, with vegan ice cream or cream or, for vegetarians, thick cream or yogurt.

Dreamy raspberry and rose pavlova

PREPARATION 20 MINUTES COOKING 1¼ HOURS SERVES 6

4 EGG WHITES • 250g (8oz) CASTER SUGAR • 2 TEASPOONS CORNFLOUR • 1 TEASPOON RED OR WHITE WINE VINEGAR, • 1 TEASPOON VANILLA EXTRACT • 300ml (½ pint) DOUBLE CREAM • 2 TEASPOONS TRIPLE-DISTILLED ROSEWATER • 375g (12oz) RASPBERRIES • A FEW RED OR PINK ROSE PETALS AND ICING SUGAR, TO DECORATE

1 Cover a large baking sheet with a piece of nonstick baking paper.

2 Make sure that the bowl and whisk you intend to use for the egg whites are both spotlessly clean and grease-free, then add the egg whites and whisk until they stand in peaks.

3 Mix together the caster sugar and cornflour, then add to the egg whites in 2 or 3 batches, whisking all the time to achieve a beautiful, glossy white meringue mixture. Finally, stir in the wine vinegar and vanilla extract.

4 Spoon the mixture on to the baking paper, gently spreading it out into a circle 20–23cm (8–9 inches) in diameter. Place in a preheated oven, 180°C (350°F), Gas Mark 4, turn the heat down to 150°C (300°F), Gas Mark 2 and bake for 1¼ hours, or until crisp. Let it cool in the oven if possible.

5 To finish the pavlova, whip the double cream until it forms soft peaks, then whisk in the rosewater. Heap this on top of the pavlova, cover with the raspberries and shower with rose petals. Serve as soon as possible, though it's still easy to eat even after 24 hours.

This pavlova looks sensational yet is easy to make. You can even make it in advance and freeze it in a rigid container. To use, put on a serving dish and allow 1–2 hours to defrost before decorating.

Notes on ingredients

Curry leaves Can be found in some large supermarkets and Indian food shops.

Daikon A large tapered white radish with a slightly hot flavour, available from supermarkets and Asian shops. Turnip can be substituted.

Eggs Use free-range, preferably organic, eggs.

Epazote A herb with a pungent, savoury flavour, often used in Mexican bean recipes to make the beans less wind-inducing. Dried epazote can be found in Mexican shops. The herb savory, which is said to have the same effect, can be substituted, or mixed herbs can be used for flavour.

Gram, or chickpea, flour A type of flour made from chickpeas. Available in large supermarkets, Indian and Middle Eastern shops.

Hoisin sauce A thick, brown, sweet and savoury sauce available from supermarkets and Chinese shops.

Ketjap manis An Indonesian soy sauce, which is sweeter and less salty than other types. Alternatively, you can sweeten ordinary soy sauce with some honey.

Kombu Dried seaweed used for the preparation of Japanese stock. Available in Asian stores and health food shops.

Kuzu (Japanese starch) Available in Japanese and health food shops. Arrowroot or cornflour can be used instead.

Lemon grass Long, tapering grass-like stalks with a lemon flavour. Crush and cook in the recipe then remove before serving, or remove the tough outer skin and use just the tender centre part, sliced.

Mirin A sweet fortified yellow Japanese wine used only for cooking. Found in Asian stores and some large supermarkets.

Miso Fermented soya paste. Generally speaking, the lighter the miso the milder the flavour and greater the sweetness. Available in health food shops and Asian stores. Buy 'unpasteurized' miso and do not boil or overheat it so as to retain health-giving enzymes.

Nori Seaweed, sold in flat sheets, for use in sushi rolls. Buy pretoasted nori from Asian and health food shops.

Palm sugar A brown, unrefined sugar used throughout Asia. It is available from large supermarkets and is often sold as a solid block. Use soft dark brown muscovado sugar as a substitute.

Rice vinegar A light, delicate vinegar made from rice wine. Available in large supermarkets and Asian shops. Wine vinegar (red or white) can be substituted, but a little less should be used.

Sake A pale golden wine made from rice, with 15–17% alcohol. Available in Asian shops. White wine or dry sherry can be substituted.

Shiitake mushrooms Chinese mushrooms, available fresh from many supermarkets and Asian shops.

Soy sauce Use a good-quality type that doesn't contain caramel, colouring, flavouring or MSG (monosodium glutamate). Tamari and Shoyu are excellent Japanese varieties.

Soya flour A type of flour made from soya beans. Available in supermarkets and health food shops.

Tamarind A long brown pod with seeds and a tangy pulp used throughout Asia as a souring ingredient. Tamarind paste can be found in jars in Indian food shops and large supermarkets. Lemon juice can be used instead.

Tempeh A naturally fermented soya product, like tofu, but made from whole soya beans, rather than soya milk. Pale-coloured tempeh is usually the best to start with as it has the mildest flavour. Available in health food shops.

Teriyaki sauce A sweet sauce made from equal parts of soy sauce and mirin (or soy sauce, sake and sugar to taste). It is available in supermarkets and Asian shops, or you can mix your own.

Thai curry paste Most contain shrimp or other fish paste but vegetarian red curry paste is available in some supermarkets.

Tofu There are several kinds of tofu available, including fresh white tofu and ready-fried tofu. It is worth trying different types to find out which you prefer. Asian (preferably Japanese) tofu, which is delicate and almost 'wobbly' in consistency, is particularly good. It is available in Asian shops.

Wasabi A strong green Japanese horseradish condiment with a hot mustard taste. It is available as a powder or a paste in large supermarkets and Asian shops. English mustard can be substituted.

Alcoholic drinks

Some wines and alcoholic drinks are prepared using animal by-products such as gelatine, although increasingly many are vegetarian or vegan. Read the label or check with the supplier to be sure. Contact the Vegetarian Society for more information.

(V) Making recipes vegan

Over one-third of the recipes in this book are naturally vegan and are labelled as such. Many more can easily be made vegan by making simple substitutions. For instance:

Little lemon cheesecakes with blueberries (see page 31)
Use margarine for the crust. Omit the double cream and lemon juice and replace with vegan cream cheese.
Lentil shepherd's pie with smoky cheese mash (see page 42)
Mash the potatoes with olive oil. Use grated smoked tofu instead of smoked cheese.
Kedgeree with quails' eggs and tarragon butter (see page 44)
Omit the eggs and replace the butter with vegan margarine.
Tamari-flavoured nut roast with tomato sauce (see page 49)
Replace the egg with 1 tablespoon of soya flour and 2 tablespoons of water.
Rocket, avocado and pine nut salad (see page 74)
Omit the pecorino cheese.
Chilli kulfi (see page 132)
Use soya cream instead of dairy cream, but reduce the amount of sugar if you are using sweetened soya cream.
Grilled polenta with roasted tomatoes (see page 153)
Omit the cheese or replace it with lots of chopped parsley.
Red lentil and roasted pepper soup (see page 170)
Omit the Parmesan shavings.

Suggested vegan alternatives

Non-vegan	Vegan
butter	vegan margarine
milk	soya milk
cream	soya cream
yogurt	soya yogurt
cream cheese	vegan cream cheese
goats' cheese	vegan cream cheese
feta	vegan feta
Cheddar (or other firm) cheese	vegan Cheddar (or other firm) cheese
Parmesan cheese (grated)	vegan Parmesan cheese
paneer	firm tofu or firm vegan cheese
mayonnaise	vegan mayonnaise
hollandaise sauce	vegan mayonnaise
honey	maple syrup

Index

A

almond and lemon cake 28
apple sauce, rosti with 70
artichokes: artichoke and green olive 'cake' 180
    artichoke heart and basil frittata 73
asparagus, croustade of 21
aubergines: Moroccan-flavoured aubergine Wellington 181
    oven-baked ratatouille 39
    puffy aubergine pancakes 12
avocados: fruity guacamole 36
    rocket, avocado and pine nut salad 74

B

bananas: banana curry 64
    banana-sesame fritters 137
    whiskey cream banoffi 53
beans: chunky bean and vegetable soup 85
    refried beans 118
    South American pinto and pumpkin casserole 119
    spicy bean cakes 143
    three-bean chilli 43
beetroot: iced beetroot soup 10
    Stilton pâté with roasted baby beetroots 154
baguettes, toasted Camembert 141
broccoli: sesame-roasted tofu with 60
    warm purple-sprouting broccoli caesar 38
butter bean and herb mash 88
butternut squash with porcini and garlic stuffing 174

C

cabbage: tagliatelle of cabbage 92
    Thai-flavoured slaw 97
cakes 28, 163
cappuccino meringues 101
carrots: carrot and caraway soup 84
    spicy vegan carrot cake 163
cashew korma 116
cauliflower: cauliflower mash 99
    cauliflower 'rice' 93
    creamy three-cheese cauliflower 71
celeriac mash 174
cheese: chargrilled artichoke heart and basil frittata 73
    cheese and sun-blush tomato muffins 157
    courgette, ricotta and petit pois lasagne 50
    creamy three-cheese cauliflower 71
    crunchy hazelnut croquettes 17
    goats' cheese and cranberry parcels 15
    haloumi with lime vinaigrette 161
    lentil shepherd's pie with smoky cheese mash 42
    Parmesan crisps 23
    ricotta 'cake' 183
    rocket, avocado and pine nut salad 74
    soft polenta with leeks and dolcelatte 58

    Stilton pâté 154
    toasted Camembert open baguettes 141
    tomato, pesto and mozzarella tart 22
    twice-baked cheese soufflés 13
    whole baked Brie in filo 175
    wild mushroom roulade 173
cheesecakes, little lemon 31
cherries: waffles with black cherry sauce 167
chestnuts: chestnut-stuffed onions 18
    chunky lentil, onion and chestnut loaf 96
chickpeas: chickpea tagine 129
    falafel with lemon sauce 131
    red pepper hummus 37
chilli: chilli kulfi 132
    three-bean chilli 43
chocolate ice cream 29
Christmas galette 178
coconut and honey ice cream 137
coffee: cappuccino meringues 101
    espresso risotto 134
coulibiac 108
courgette, ricotta and petit pois lasagne 50
couscous, chickpea tagine with 129
curries 64, 116

D

daikon: no-rice nori sushi 34

E

eggs: chargrilled artichoke heart and basil frittata 73
    eggs in coconut curry sauce 93
    eggy tomatoes with garlic and basil 151
    kedgeree with eggs and tarragon butter 44
    see also omelettes
espresso risotto 134

F

falafel with lemon sauce 131
fennel, lentil and olive pâté with 156
figs, vanilla-poached 102
frittata 73
fritters 128, 137

G

goats' cheese and cranberry parcels 15
grapes: quinoa and red grape salad 98
guacamole, fruity 36

H

hazelnuts: crispy nut balls 148
    crunchy hazelnut croquettes 17
honey and ginger pashka 135
hummus, red pepper 37

I

ice cream 29, 137
Indonesian savoury stuffed pineapples 124

J

Japanese layered-omelette slices 150

K

kedgeree with eggs and tarragon butter 44
kulfi, chilli 132

L

laksa 63
lasagne: courgette, ricotta and petit pois 50
leeks, soft polenta with dolcelatte and 58
lemon cheesecakes 31
lentils: chunky lentil, onion and chestnut loaf 96
    kedgeree with eggs and tarragon butter 44
    lentil and olive pâté 156
    lentil shepherd's pie 42
    lentils with portobellos, garlic and red wine 89
    red lentil and roasted pepper soup 170
    sweet potato and coconut dal 115

M

mango, cardamom and pistachio fool 78
maple syrup pudding 81
mascarpone, amaretti and raspberry trifles 77
Mediterranean stuffed peppers 99
melon, strawberry and mint compôte 162
meringues 101, 187
Moroccan-flavoured aubergine Wellington 181
muffins 157
mushrooms: baby potatoes and mushrooms 144
    coulibiac 108
    laksa 63
    lentils with portobellos, garlic and red wine 89
    Thai-flavoured mushroom stroganoff 41
    twice-baked cheese soufflés on mushroom steaks 13
    wild mushroom roulade 173

N

noodles: laksa 63
    vegetarian pad thai 111
nori sushi, no-rice 34
nut roast, tamari-flavoured 49

O

okra with red onions, mustard seeds and brown rice 86
olives: artichoke and green olive 'cake' 180
    lentil and olive pâté 156
    spaghetti with black olive and tomato sauce 67
omelettes: Japanese layered-omelette slices 150
    omelette cannelloni with spinach filling 94
onions: chestnut-stuffed onions 18
    sage, onion and apple sausages 142
orange salad, Moroccan 28

P

pad thai, vegetarian 111

pak choi, butter bean and herb mash with 88
pakora vegetables 125
pancakes, puffy aubergine 12
paneer, tandoori 126
pashka, honey and ginger 135
pastries 15, 108, 175, 181
pâtés 154, 156
pavlova 187
peaches: fruity guacamole 36
peas: courgette, ricotta and petit pois lasagne 50
    pea and mint timbales 23
peppers: Mediterranean stuffed 99
    oven-baked ratatouille 39
    puffy aubergine pancakes with red pepper purée 12
    red lentil and roasted pepper soup 170
    red pepper hummus 37
    three-bean chilli with multi-coloured peppers 43
pie, luscious vegan pumpkin 184
pineapples: grilled pineapple with palm sugar and
        crème fraîche 164
    Indonesian savoury stuffed 124
polenta: grilled polenta with roasted tomatoes 153
    soft polenta with leeks and dolcelatte 58
pomegranate: fruity guacamole 36
potatoes: baby potatoes and mushrooms 144
    celeriac mash 174
    lentil shepherd's pie 42
    rosti with apple sauce 70
pumpkin: luscious vegan pumpkin pie 184
    South American pinto and pumpkin casserole 119

Q

quinoa and red grape salad 98

R

raspberries: dreamy raspberry and rose pavlova 187
    mascarpone, amaretti and raspberry trifles 77
ratatouille, oven-baked 39
rice: banana curry with cashew rice 64
    chilled rosewater rice pudding 54
    coulibiac 108
    espresso risotto 134
    green risotto 91
    Indonesian savoury stuffed pineapples 124
    kedgeree with eggs and tarragon butter 44
    spicy okra with red onions, mustard seeds and brown rice 86
    sweet potato and wild rice patties 16
    Thai-flavoured mushroom stroganoff with golden rice 41
ricotta 'cake' 183
rocket, avocado and pine nut salad 74
rosewater rice pudding 54
rosti with apple sauce 70

S

salads: quinoa and red grape 98
    rocket, avocado and pine nut 74
    Thai-flavoured slaw 97
    warm purple-sprouting broccoli caesar 38
sausages, sage, onion and apple 142
sesame-roasted tofu 60

shepherd's pie 42
soufflés, twice-baked cheese 13
soups: carrot and caraway 84
    chunky bean and vegetable 85
    iced beetroot 10
    laksa 63
    red lentil and roasted pepper 170
South American pinto and pumpkin casserole 119
spaghetti with black olive and tomato sauce 67
spinach: omelette cannelloni with spinach filling 94
    tagliatelle with creamy spinach and nutmeg sauce 66
spring rolls, Vietnamese 121
strawberry, honeydew melon and mint compôte 162
sushi, no-rice nori 34
sweet potatoes: sweet potato and coconut dal 115
    sweet potato and wild rice patties 16
sweetcorn: corn fritters with tomato sauce 128

T
tagliatelle with creamy spinach and nutmeg sauce 66
tamari-flavoured nut roast 49
tandoori paneer 126
tarts 22, 178
tempeh, crisp-fried 59
Thai-flavoured mushroom stroganoff 41
Thai-flavoured slaw 97
tofu: agedashi tofu 114
    luscious vegan pumpkin pie 184
    sesame-roasted tofu 60
    stir-fry with sizzling tofu 24
    vegetarian pad thai 111
tomatoes: cheese and sun-blush tomato muffins 157
    eggy tomatoes 151
    grilled polenta with roasted tomatoes 153
    spaghetti with black olive and tomato sauce 67
    tamari-flavoured nut roast with tomato sauce 49
    tomato, pesto and mozzarella tart 22
trifles 77

V
vegan recipes 189
vegetables: Christmas galette 178
    chunky bean and vegetable soup 85
    green risotto 91
    pakora vegetables 125
    ricotta 'cake' with honey- and cardamom-roasted
      vegetables 183
    stir-fry with sizzling tofu 24
    see also individual types of vegetable
Vietnamese spring rolls 121

W
waffles with black cherry sauce 167
whiskey cream banoffi 53
wild rice and sweet potato patties 16

Acknowledgements

Many talented people have been involved with the production of this book, and I'd like to acknowledge them all. In particular, Sarah Ford, commissioning editor, who had the initial idea, masterminded the project and generously shared many mouthwatering ideas; Alison Goff, publisher, Sue Bobbermein, publicity manager, and Clare Churly, managing editor, who were also in at the very beginning; Tracy Killick, creative director, for creating so completely the kind of look I wanted (and for making me laugh); to all who were involved with the photo shoots: Gus Filgate – a huge 'thank you', you were brilliant – David Morgan for showing off the food at its absolute best and for contributing some lovely ideas. Thanks also to Jo MacGregor, designer, for her unfailing eye and Rachel Lawrence, editor, who has been a joy to work with; Stephen McIlmoyle for making me look my best for the photos and Liz Hippisley for the beautiful props. Thanks too to Barbara Dixon for meticulous copy-editing (so good to work with you again, Barbara); my daughter Claire for tasting (special thank you), my agent, Barbara Levy; my husband Robert for mammoth washing up sessions and much besides. Thank you all.

Executive Editor Sarah Ford
Senior Editor Rachel Lawrence
Executive Art Editor Joanna MacGregor
Design Grade Design Consultants, London
Picture Research Jennifer Veall
Production Controller Martin Croshaw

Special photography Gus Filgate
Food stylist David Morgan
Prop stylist Liz Hippisley

With grateful thanks to David Mellor kitchen suppliers, for the loan of cutlery, china and glassware.
www.davidmellordesign.co.uk 020 7730 4259